Netiquette:
Internet etiquette in the age of the blog

By Matthew Strawbridge

Published by Software Reference Ltd

Copyright © 2006 Matthew Strawbridge

10 09 08 07 06

10 9 8 7 6 5 4 3 2 1

British Library Cataloguing in Publication Data is available from the British Library on request.

10-digit ISBN: 0 9554614 0 5

13-digit ISBN: 978 0 9554614 0 8

Disclaimers

Product and company names mentioned herein may be trademarks of their respective owners.

None of the content of this book is intended as legal advice. The author and publisher accept no responsibility for any loss sustained as a result of the contents or any errors or omissions of this book.

Acknowledgements

The author would like to thank the following people for their contributions to this book: Justin Hayward, John Westwood, Jim Strawbridge and Richard Knowles.

Proofread by Rod Cuff, Word & Web (UK) Ltd.

Contents

❧ 1. Introduction ❧

Who should read this book?

The short answer: anyone who uses the Internet.

The long answer: Internet users who want to act responsibly, and to be seen to act responsibly, on the Internet. The ironic thing is that those who could benefit the most from reading this book – the minority who stomp about cyberspace with a total disregard for other people – are the least likely to do so. In contrast, you – literate, keen to learn, and willing to think and discuss – need only polish your already good behaviour. I hope that you will learn some useful tips, as I have done when preparing this material.

What is netiquette?

Etiquette

Netiquette is a specific type of etiquette. Etiquette is the framework of formal rules and customs governing how people behave: a description of what constitutes good manners. The historical reasons for etiquette are many and varied. Etiquette may be born of superstition (it would be rude to say 'Macbeth' in a theatre) or religious belief, of cultural heritage or general common sense. Whatever the reason, the rules of etiquette are designed as a 'think before you act' reminder to prevent you from causing discomfort to other people. By conforming to the rules of etiquette, you automatically benefit from a raised level of humility and empathy; if everyone does this, communication becomes easier and people aren't needlessly injured by the fallout from stray remarks.

Etiquette in the Internet age

Different cultures have different established rules of etiquette. For example, burping after a meal is generally considered to be impolite in the Western world, yet in some other cultures this is seen as praise for the chef and an indication that you enjoyed the meal.

There is a similar discrepancy between what is considered to be appropriate behaviour online compared with the 'real world'. The difference is clear from the way that so-called **newbies**, who have yet to adapt to the protocols of online communication, can frustrate experienced users of the Internet by inappropriate behaviour.

> **Newbies** are new users – either new to the Internet in general, or just new to a particular forum.

This **network etiquette** has been shortened to **netiquette**. The *Oxford English Dictionary* defines netiquette as 'an informal code of practice regulating the behaviour of Internet users when using e-mail, bulletin boards, chat rooms, newsgroups, etc.' and traces the word's history back to 1982.

The Internet is still primarily a text-based medium. Communication by writing has always been governed by a loose set of rules and guidelines, which tend to become tighter in proportion to the formality of the purpose of the writing; formal letters tend to obey stricter guidelines than internal memos, for example. In common with other written forms of communication, messages on the Internet lack the supporting framework of 'tone of voice'; this missing element can make it more difficult to get a message across clearly. Because of this, there is an increased danger of misinterpretation and of dialogues descending into unproductive 'flame wars' (see page 111).

History

When the Internet was in its infancy, its citizens were mainly academics and technology enthusiasts. Since then, it has grown at a phenomenal rate. The Internet is shaped by its users, and so its culture has changed from academic to popularist, from specialist to general, from expert to average as new people have started to use it. The Internet is no longer a military and academic research tool – it is a source of education and entertainment to many millions of people across the world.

The following chart shows the growth in the number of computers connected to the Internet (Internet hosts).

Internet hosts

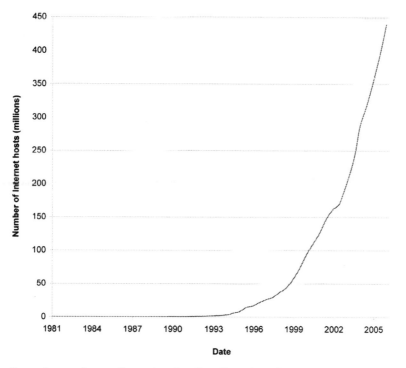

Source: Internet Systems Consortium, Inc. (http://www.isc.org)

Note that the origins of the Internet can be traced back to the 1960s – see (Leiner, et al., 2003) for more information.

Both the amount of information carried and the number of users have increased exponentially, and show no signs of slowing down. This growth has brought many opportunities, as well as some additional threats –

spam (page 93), phishing (page 104), quick-spreading viruses (page 101) and so on – that were unimagined in the Internet's early days.

About this book

Motivation

I used to work as a software engineer. The company I worked for had a standards document for the language in which I was programming: C++. This document was very terse and dry, and although all the software engineers were supposed to be following it to the letter, the rules were difficult to understand and to remember.

At around this time I discovered a copy of (Henricson & Nyquist, 1992) on the Internet. The subject matter of this document is the same – a list of rules to follow in order to write good, maintainable computer programs – but I found the presentation style to be far superior. The fundamental difference was that each rule was accompanied by an explanation of why you should follow it. If you disagree with the rationale, perhaps you need not follow the rule (or at least could put forward an argument explaining why you think the rule should be changed). I learned a great deal about C++ from reading this document; my programming ability improved not because of the set of rules I was asked to follow, but because of a totally separate set of rules that were backed up with concrete examples of their use and misuse.

Although this book is very different from a style guide for a programming language, I hope that I have managed to incorporate those elements that made the second C++ guide better than the first. For each of the rules I have suggested, I have given an explanation of why I think it is a good idea – you are welcome to disagree, but at least you should understand my motivation for including it.

Structure

This book is split into three parts.

The first part is named *Forms of Online Communication* and covers the netiquette of communication over the Internet, with chapters devoted to email, real-time messages, and various other forms of online discussion.

The second part of the book is named *Online Services* and introduces some rules covering our interactions as users with some common types of service that are hosted online, particularly on the World Wide Web.

The final part of the book comprises the rules and recommendations that are important to netiquette but are not related to specific forms of communication or online services. As a result, this part is called *Other Issues*. The topics discussed in this part of the book include online security and spam.

Cross-references

References to other sources are in the form (Author, Year). Further information on these is given in the bibliography on page 151.

References to rules are given in the form *#nn*, where *nn* is the rule number. A summary of the rules, including the page numbers on which they appear, is given in Appendix C (page 125).

Learning some lessons

Most books about computers age very quickly as new hardware, software and the ways in which they are used come in. Books about young technologies face even quicker redundancy. However, the basic principles laid down here – mostly examples of treating others as you would like to be treated – will continue to be relevant for a long time to come.

I hope that I have argued the case for the rules presented here. They are a combination of established practice and common sense. I haven't dreamt them up just to make life difficult for you. In fact, when you are at your keyboard, I won't be standing behind you with a big stick forcing you to follow the rules. Neither is this an attempt to stifle individuality or creativity, as can often be the case with 'political correctness' mandates. Rather, I hope that this book gives you enough background information to enable you to make an informed decision whenever you choose to break these rules!

Matthew Strawbridge
November 2006

PART 1 – FORMS OF ONLINE COMMUNICATION

2.   Email

Email is perhaps the most widespread form of communication on the Internet. It is certainly one of the oldest. As well as being used to send simple messages, the email system is often integral to other forms of Internet communication, such as mailing lists. As a result, many of the rules presented here will also be applicable elsewhere on the Internet, but aren't repeated in later chapters.

Structure and style

Openings and closings

There is an established etiquette in letter writing concerning the choice of opening (**Dear ...**) and closing (**Yours ...**). Normally, for business letters, this should be as follows:

Description	Opening	Closing
Formal letter to someone whose name you do not know	Dear Sir/Madam	Yours faithfully
Formal letter to someone whose name you do know	Dear Mr Smith	Yours sincerely
Informal letter to someone with whom you are on first-name terms	Dear John	**Kind regards** or **Best wishes** or **Yours**

The equivalents for email communications are less clear-cut. An email is usually less formal than a letter – more at the level of a telephone call. Most of the emails I write start with the form **Hi John*** and end with **Best wishes.**

---

* This seems friendlier than starting simply 'John', as some people do. However, it does run the risk of coming across as over-familiar, so use your discretion based on what you know about the person you are writing to. Perhaps **Hello** would be better than **Hi**. For a business email, it is safer to use the same type of opening as you would for a letter, especially when contacting someone for the first time, so use your judgement. An unusual opening or closing will only cause distraction.

If someone signs an email with his or her given name (e.g. 'Regards, Matthew'), or even with an abbreviation (e.g. 'Regards, Matt'), it is fine to use that in the opening to your reply, even if you do not know that person very well. When doing this, make sure that you get the person's name right – I often get emails addressed to 'Mathew' or even, occasionally, to 'Martin'!

Structure

1. **Each line should be a maximum of 65 characters wide.**

   This recommendation is given in (Hambridge & Intel, 1995). Other sources give longer recommended line lengths, such as 70 characters. The reason for this rule is that email reader software will attempt to wrap long lines. Suppose you send your emails with a line width of 80 characters, and your recipient's software is set up to wrap at 65 characters – they will end up with pairs of long and short lines alternating all the way down the page.

   Most software for sending emails will do this line wrapping automatically; just make sure that yours does, too.

2. **Structure your message using paragraphs and sentences of sensible lengths.**

   This rule is simply good writing style. Very long paragraphs and sentences will be difficult to read, and information is likely to get skipped or misunderstood. Press **Enter** twice between paragraphs so that there is a full blank line between each – this will make your message look better, and the structure will be clear.

Style

3. **Avoid non-standard forms of English, such as txt or l33t.**

   This rule probably goes without saying to anyone over the age of 15. Emails should almost always use standard English rather than the contractions of text messages or the obfuscated l33t beloved of certain groups on the Internet. This rule might seem redundant at first, but it's not uncommon to see emails with subjects such as 'hlp pls'. Although the meaning is fairly clear, only three letters have been saved, and the recipient is required to spend a little extra time thinking.

> When I say **txt**, I mean the forms of abbreviation, such as **CUL8R** for 'see you later', used in SMS text messages.
>
> Leet (also known as **1337** or l33t) is a simple cipher on the Internet, in which letters are replaced by numbers or other symbols. The term **leet** itself is a corruption of **elite**, typically applied to a hacker with good skills. Wikipedia has a fuller description: (Wikipedia, 2006, December 5).

In 2003, a 13-year-old Scottish girl reportedly wrote an entire English essay in txt because it was 'easier than standard English' (BBC, 2003). The beginning of the essay was as follows:

My smmr hols wr CWOT. B4, we used 2go2 NY 2C my bro, his GF & 3 :- kids FTF. ILNY, it's a gr8 plc.

meaning

My summer holidays were a complete waste of time. Before, we used to go to New York to see my brother, his girlfriend and their three screaming kids face to face. I love New York. It's a great place.

There have been other reports of youngsters using this style of writing for their answers in exams (BBC, 2002). This is clearly an extreme case, but it could be an indication of a trend.

11

Signatures

4. **If you have a signature automatically appended to every email you send, keep its length to a maximum of six (preferably four) lines of 70 characters each.**

    A **signature** (or **sig** for short) is rather like headed notepaper. Its fundamental purpose is to give enough information for the recipient to be able to contact you. These days, a web address is probably sufficient – your website is a more appropriate place to provide details about the myriad ways in which you can be contacted (telephone, fax, carrier pigeon...). However, you may also wish to provide your email address (some email software will strip this out); you could mung it (see page 51) to protect you from spam.

    It might be acceptable to include a short witty quotation or joke in your sig, but consider whether this will just become noise to the reader if you never change it. In addition, consider whether everyone shares your sense of humour – in particular, you don't want to cause offence. (Harris, 2006) suggests avoiding sig content relating to religion, race, politics or sexuality, or to local or topical subjects that not everyone will 'get'.

    You really don't want your signature to distract the reader from the content of your message, so large **ASCII art** pictures are a bad idea (compounded by the fact that people who choose not to use a fixed-width font will not be able to see them

> ASCII is the American Standard Code for Information Interchange, which maps letters and symbols to the numbers used to represent them in a computer. **ASCII art** is the term used to describe pictures made up of these letters and symbols. Most ASCII art must be viewed in a fixed-width font to make sense.

anyway). (Horton, Spafford, & Moraes, 1998) says 'DO NOT include drawings, pictures, maps, or other graphics in your signature – it is not the appropriate place for such material and is viewed as rude by other readers.'

It is a convention to start a signature with a single line containing just two hyphens. The idea is that this allows email and mailing list software to detect where a signature starts, perhaps removing it if it is too long.

Some companies automatically append lengthy legal disclaimers to every email message that is sent. This is rarely done for the benefit of the recipient, and such boilerplate text can often overpower a shorter email message. I am not a lawyer, but I would suggest that a simple disclaimer referring the recipient to a fuller version on the company website would confer the same protection without causing as much irritation. After all, very few companies insist that their employees launch into a legalese script whenever they make a telephone call – the people being called wouldn't put up with this behaviour, so they shouldn't be subjected to the same thing in text form.

Sig examples

Good

```
--
Bob Widget
Acme Internet Services
<http://www.example.com>
```

Bad

```
****   ***   ****         *   *  *****  ****    ****  *****  *****
*   *  *   *  *   *  *     *   *    *    *   *  *      *        *
****   *   *  ****        * * *     *    *   *  * **   ***      *
*   *  *   *  *   *  *     * *      *    *   *  *  *   *        *
****   ***   ****          * *    *****  ****    ***  *****     *

**************************************************************
*                                                          *
*     A   C   M   E     I   N   T   E   R   N   E   T       *
*       S     E   R   V   I   C   E   S                     *
*                                                          *
**************************************************************
```

This might appear as follows if the recipient uses a proportional font:

```
****   ***  ****      *  * ***** ****   **** ***** *****
*  *   *  *  *         *  *  *   *  *  *     *       *
****   *  *  ****      *** *   *  * * *  **  ***     *
*  *   *  *  *         **  *   *  *  * *   *       *
****   ***  ****       * * ***** ****   *** *****   *
```

```
****************************************************************
*                                       *
*    A C M E   I N T E R N E T    *
*    S E R V I C E S        *
*                          *
****************************************************************
```

Tone and content

5. **Use an appropriate level of small talk.**

    Consider what you would say if you were telephoning the person instead of emailing. You would be unlikely to get straight to the business at hand – there would probably be some 'how are the family' discussion beforehand, even if it is very short. This might seem frivolous, but it helps to build rapport, and gives both parties a little time to 'get their brains in gear'.

    You wouldn't want to ramble on for pages talking about the weather in a business email, but a small amount of padding can help to lighten the mood and ensure that you are seen to be approachable. This is particularly important if there is any negative content to the rest of your message, because it will act as a buffer and help to balance the tone (although, if your message will be too negative, perhaps email is not the best way to put it across – see #8). To make this extra material meaningful, try to tailor it to the individual and to vary it over time – simply saying 'I hope you are well' at the start of each email is likely to bring on a bout of hypochondria!

6. **Keep business emails short and to the point.**

    Respect other people's time. Take the effort to marshal your thoughts before putting finger to keyboard. As a result, your message will be clearer and better received.

> *I would have written a shorter letter, but I did not have the time.*
>
> Blaise Pascal (1623–1662)
> French mathematician, physicist, and theologian

7. **Think carefully before sending an email that could embarrass you if it were to be more widely distributed.**

    An alternative way of saying this is 'Do not send information by email that you wouldn't shout in a crowded room.' This long-standing advice serves as a reminder that it is trivially easy for the recipient of an email you send to forward it to someone else. There have been many reported instances of people being publicly humiliated and losing their jobs as a result of a hastily sent email being more widely distributed than they had expected it to be.

8. **Do not use email to send bad news.**

    If you need to break bad news, a face-to-face meeting is best. This allows both parties the benefit of reacting to the full range of visual and aural signals given out by the other person. If this is not possible, a telephone call is next best.

    There have even been reports of staff being notified of their redundancies by email or pager message, some examples of which are given overleaf.

In 2003, the UK's largest personal injuries claim firm, The Accident Group (TAG), went into administration. At that time, 2400 employees received a series of text messages to their mobile phones, informing them that they had lost their jobs and that their last month's salary would not be paid. A test case involving 21 of those employees was brought to court in December 2003; they won a 'protection award' from the Government amounting to £260 per week for 90 days' work in lieu of notice, after it was found that 'the staff had been cynically manipulated to keep the company running until the last possible moment'. This is somewhat ironic given that the company's catchphrase was 'Where there's blame, there's a claim'!

An earlier example is given by *The Register* website (McCarthy, 2001). In February 2001, office administrator Zoe Halls is reported to have been sacked from her probationary job by her boss, who sent the message, 'We don't need you in at work tomorrow, I'll phone you AM to explain – John.'

9.   **Do not write all in capital (or all in lower-case) letters.**

Some people, typically 'hunt and peck' typists, write entirely in capital letters. Occasional and restrained use of capital letters can be useful for emphasis, but writing entirely in capitals is the written equivalent of shouting. Writing any message entirely in a single case makes it difficult to read.

THIS TEXT IS ALL IN CAPITAL LETTERS. IT IS LIKE SHOUTING AND IS DIFFICULT TO READ.

this text is all in lowercase letters. it looks amateurish and is also difficult to read.

This text is in proper sentences. It is easier to read than it would be if it were all in a single case.

10. **Do not use email as a way to avoid social interaction.**

Believe it or not, some people have been known to send email to the person sitting right next to them, just to ask a simple question that they could have asked verbally. This behaviour is an extreme form of a more common problem: using emails to the exclusion of all other forms of communication.

Email use is not the only problem here: some people rely too heavily on telephone communication, for example, even for low-priority matters that might be better dealt with via email. In a modern working environment, we have an array of communication tools to choose from: face-to-face meetings, letters, faxes, telephone conversations, and, yes, emails. The professional thing to do is to choose the best tool for the job, rather than simply relying on the one with which you are most comfortable.

11. **Read your emails before you send them.**

It's amazing how many people seem to miss this step. What you wrote might not mean what you thought it did when you come to read it back to yourself. Taking the time to perform a quick read-through can save you from all manner of embarrassment and confusion. If you can edit the email to say the same thing in fewer words (see #6), so much the better!

12. If your email system allows you to set the priority of the emails you send, make use of this facility (in particular, mark low-priority emails).

Some people may have their email readers set up to make a sound whenever they receive email, but not to do this for low-priority emails. By correctly marking any low-priority emails you send, you will help such people by not interrupting their work.

13. Wrap URLs in angle brackets, like this: <http://www.example.com/whatever.html>.

Wrapping URLs in angle brackets highlights them and makes it easy to separate them from any surrounding punctuation. Including **http://** at the front makes it more likely that the recipient's email client will make the link clickable, instead of the recipient having to cut and paste it into a web browser.

14. **Take care when using terms that might get your message misidentified as spam.**

(Kallos, 2004) goes so far as to recommend that you use asterisks to break up such danger words, for example by typing **fr*ee** instead of **free**. To me, this is a step too far. Any spam filter that rejects such a common word is effectively broken. However, if you are sending something particularly important, or if you know that the recipient has a particularly zealous spam filter, this might be your only option. See Chapter 10 for a full discussion of spam.

Here are some words that you should be aware might trigger spam filters: **casino, cheap, credit card, degree, finances, free, pharmacy, pill, sex** and any obscenities. There are, of course, hundreds of others, and any decent spam filter will take account of various other factors before designating any given email as spam.

Subject lines

Meaningful subjects

15. **Use a sufficiently long subject so that people will have an accurate idea about your email's contents.**

    People shouldn't have to open your message in order to know what it is about. This is particularly important if you are sending it to a large number of people, some of whom may have only a passing interest in the details (although this might represent a problem in itself, as explained in #17). In particular, if you don't type a subject at all then your email is much more likely to be accidentally deleted as suspected spam without being opened. Remember that people may need to refer back to your email at a later date, so avoid generic subjects such as 'Here is the report' which, although they may make sense while previous conversations are fresh in the recipient's mind, will be meaningless in a few weeks.

    However, do not go to the other extreme of trying to get all the information across in the subject – this is what the body of the message is for.

Threading

16. **Only change subject lines when it is helpful to other people to do so (using [long] and [was ...]).**

    Suppose your anti-spam software adds [spam] to the subject line of emails that it suspects to be spam; when you reply to a legitimate email that has been incorrectly marked as spam, you should delete this extra content from the subject line. In contrast, if you are writing a particularly long response to a short email, it is polite to alert people to this fact by adding [long] to the subject (although this is perhaps less important now that fast Internet connections are commonplace). Marking long messages is particularly important in discussion lists, so this has a rule of its own in that part of the book (see #48).

It is quite usual for email discussions to veer off from the original subject. In such cases, it is helpful to identify both the new and old topics of conversation. An example would be 'Price of fish [was Haddock pie]', where a conversation has changed from an exchange of recipes for haddock pie to a lament at the high price of fish. For another example, see the illustration of threading in #22.

Recipients

17. **Send messages to only those people who are likely to want to read them.**

Many people use the CC mechanism to distribute their messages to people other than the primary recipient 'just in case'. Managers are probably the main sufferers of being excessively copied in. Sometimes the only reason for this is a misguided attempt by the sender to impress them or to impress other recipients by their inclusion in the distribution.

> CC stands for **carbon copy**, dating from the days where copies of a letter or memo could be made using carbon paper. In terms of email, users can be sent copies of an email addressed to someone else by adding their email addresses to the CC field.
>
> A **BCC (blind carbon copy)** can be used to send copies of an email without the official recipients knowing.

Although CCs can often be useful, many businesses, in particular, suffer from an excess of emails. Some companies have suffered to such an extent that they have stopped using emails altogether for internal communication.

Perhaps the most famous example of a company cutting out email is that of Phones4U, a UK-based mobile phone retailer. Back in 2003, John Cauldwell, then Director of Phones4U, who himself doesn't use email, placed an informal ban on its use throughout the organisation. This was in response to management concerns that the growing use of emails was increasing the time it took to deal with customers' queries. Other companies have tended to take a piecemeal approach, perhaps banning emails one or two days a week.

If you routinely CC someone in to emails that they are not interested in, they may start to disregard them all. This 'crying wolf' will mean that you are likely to be ignored when you finally come to send them something urgent that they would genuinely be interested in.

If you find that you are receiving emails that you do not wish to read, politely ask the sender to remove you from the distribution in future. Encourage other people to do the same for messages you send. In a business environment, it might be more cost-effective to store widely distributed but narrowly read documents, such as meeting minutes, in a central location such as an intranet or content management system – this would enable people to search for information when they needed it, without clogging up their inboxes.

Remember that many people will save emails just in case they need to refer to them later. It is wasteful of resources to send an email to, say, 100 staff, and to have that email stored on 100 different computers. Every item of data stored on a computer will degrade its performance slightly – searches will take longer, as will administrative tasks such as virus scans and backups.

18. **Avoid using BCC unless it is clear that you have done so.**

    It is right and proper to use **BCC** to keep recipients' details private (see #37). However, using **BCC** to allow extra people to snoop on a conversation without the named recipients' knowledge is poor netiquette.

19. **Differentiate between TO and CC.**

    Use the **TO** field to list the main recipients of the email. Use **CC** to list recipients who will find the content worthwhile (in deference to #17) but from whom you don't anticipate any response.

20. **Use people's full names (in title case) as well as their email addresses in the TO, FROM and CC fields.**

    You can usually supply both the full name and email address in these fields. Using a format such as **John A. Smith <smithj@example.com>**

    > The **postmaster** is the person who administers an organisation's email system (see also pages 117–118).

    looks professional and contains all the necessary information. If you make a typo in the email, including the full name might allow the intended recipient's **postmaster** to forward the message to them anyway.

    It is always a good idea to include your own name in full in the **FROM** field, to help the recipients to identify quickly who sent them the message. As stated in (Harris, 2006), fake names such as 'Guess Who' are annoying and should be avoided.

Replying to emails

21. **Respond promptly to emails sent to you.**

Although people won't expect an instantaneous response, as a rule of thumb you should try to respond to business emails within four hours and to personal emails within a day. If you need more time to formulate a fuller response, send a brief email to say this.

22. **Use the Reply button in your email software to reply to emails – don't start a new message.**

Some people use email software that supports threads. A thread is a tree-like structure that groups together all the messages about a topic – the original message and any responses to it (and responses to those responses, and so on). Email messages use data fields to record information. Some of these fields are visible such as the **TO**, **FROM** and **SUBJECT** fields – whereas others are part of the email but are not usually displayed to the user. Some of these fields are used to control threading, so starting a fresh message will break this link and frustrate these users.

Example of threaded emails

Staff Party	Bob Smith <bob.smith@example.com>
Re: Staff Party	Sally Jenkins <sally.jenkins@example.com>
Food [was Staff Party]	Fran Carter <fran.carter@example.com>
Re: Food [was Staff Party]	Sanjay Patel <sanjay.patel@example.com>
Re: Food [was Staff Party]	Eileen Jones <eileen.jones@example.com>
Re: Staff Party	Alex Chang <alex.chang@example.com>

23. **Check with the author before adding extra recipients to a reply to an email.**

    Although the original author of the message usually won't mind your circulating their message more widely, there may be reasons why they wouldn't want particular people to read it. Also remember too that whoever writes an email has the copyright to its contents (whether or not they explicitly provide a copyright statement to that effect), and distributing that email may be an infringement of that copyright.

    See also #32, which covers the same topic with respect to forwarding emails.

24. **It is traditional to include the text of the original message in the reply, typically below the new material and distinguished in some way (such as by prepending each line with a > character). If you need to respond point-by-point, you may intersperse your comments with the original text so long as it is clear which is which.**

    Do not add your material below the original message, because this forces the recipient to scroll down unnecessarily.

    You should always include some of the original message, otherwise you are creating extra work for the reader if they need to open the original message in order to fully understand your reply. The topic will be fresh in your mind when you write your response (you will typically have just finished reading the original message), but the recipient may not get round to reading your response straight away, and is likely to have been distracted by other things in the interim.

25. **Unless you are adding further recipients to your reply, quote only as much material as is necessary to give context to your own response.**

It is reasonable to assume that the recipients of your response have already read the original email, so they will not want to read it all again. However, it is useful to provide enough context to jog their memories. This rule is particularly important for discussions containing many posts and having many participants. If you decide to remove a large portion of text, adding <snip> in its place indicates that you have read it, and that the decision to remove it was intentional (see also #33).

26. **If you set up an automatic reply for when you are on holiday, make certain that it will reply only to individuals and not to mailing lists of which you are a member.**

If you send one of these 'out of office' responses to a mailing list, you will be advertising your carelessness very publicly. However, if used correctly, these automatic response tools are useful for letting people know that you will not be able to respond immediately to whatever it is they have emailed to you.

27. **If you received an email because you were BCCed on it, and other recipients would be surprised that you had seen it, do not use 'Reply to All'.**

The BCC feature may be used for two main purposes: to protect the privacy of the recipients or to distribute information in secret. If you have received an email via the first of these routes, feel free to use 'Reply to All' (although your message will not reach any other BCCed recipients of the original message) – you are voluntarily resigning your anonymity, and this is your right. If, for whatever reason, you were sent a copy of the message without the knowledge of the original recipients, you should probably restrict any replies to the original sender (the person who added you to the distribution in the first place).

To repeat #18: there are few good reasons for using BCC surreptitiously. If what you are doing is 'sneaky' (letting someone else eavesdrop on a private conversation), you can be sure that it isn't good etiquette!

28. **Don't reply to an email just as an easy way to create a new email to the same people.**

When you need to discuss a new subject, start a new email with a new subject. Reusing an existing one is sloppy, and could confuse threaded email readers (see also #22).

29. **When replying to emails, don't send identical files back to people who already have them.**

Most email software does this for you – when you reply to an email that has an attachment, the attachment is not sent back with your reply. However, if you need to add further recipients as part of your reply, and they haven't seen the attachment, you may be inclined to attach the file. A better approach would be to forward the original email to the new recipients separately (with permission – see #32), and then to mention that you have done this when replying to the email and adding the new recipients to the distribution.

30. **Prepend the subject lines of your replies and forwarded messages with the standard two-letter designations (RE and FW respectively).**

If you use your email software's **Reply** and **Forward** commands when replying to or forwarding emails, these designations should be inserted automatically. Do not be tempted to delete them. They help the recipient of your message to understand what it is: a new message, a reply or a forwarded message. For this reason, do not add **RE** to the subject lines of new emails that you compose, even though this is common when writing memos on paper.

Forwarding emails

31. **Always add a short comment to say why you are forwarding the email.**

    When you receive an email that someone has forwarded to you, the first thing you want to know is 'What is this?' The second thing you want to know is 'Why have they sent it to me?' By adding a short note to any email that you forward to other people, you can answer both of these questions for them. Contrast this approach with simply forwarding an attachment to someone and typing 'FYI' in the body – the recipient would need to open the file to find out whether they were interested in its contents!

32. **Don't forward emails that were sent to you privately (or to a private forum of which you are a member) without the original sender's permission. This applies whether you want to send the email to another person or to a mailing list.**

    Imagine if every email you had ever sent were suddenly to be published for everyone to read online! You have probably written some things privately that you wouldn't want to be general knowledge. This is an extreme, of course, but it is a general courtesy to ask someone whether you may distribute their words more widely. There is also the matter of copyright to consider.

    Most people will actually be flattered to learn that you think that what they wrote to you will also be of interest to other people, so they generally won't have any objection to your forwarding it. However, it is still polite to ask in advance.

If someone had sent you a letter, would you photocopy it and send it to someone else without asking permission? Would you record a telephone call and then play it back to someone else? Just because it is quick and easy to forward an email, this doesn't mean that you should do so without thinking first.

See also #23, which explains why you shouldn't add extra recipients to an email when replying without first checking with the original author.

33. Do not edit the text of a forwarded email.

When you forward an email (with permission, of course, as stated in #32), you are quoting someone else. If you edit what they wrote, you risk misrepresenting them in some way, perhaps even libelling them.

If you do need to amend the text, you should make it obvious which parts were your edits. A common way to do this is to insert tags in square or angle brackets, such as [sic] to highlight a quoted mistake (use with extreme care) or <snip> to show that you have removed some of the original text (see also #25).

Hoaxes

34. Never send warnings about the latest virus by email.

If you receive an email saying something like 'Do not open any email with the subject line "important update" because it contains a virus', or advising you to search for and remove a particular file from your hard disk, there is a high probability that the email is a hoax, however well-intentioned the person who sent it to you. Do not escalate the problem by sending the email to other people.

Rely on the professional security companies that produce anti-virus tools to keep you safe. As long as you obtain frequent updates of the virus definition files (and most software does this automatically), this should be sufficient to protect you against the latest threats.

The one exception is when you know for sure that you have recently been infected by a particular virus. Then you may (indeed should) notify those people to whom you are likely to have transmitted it, apologising, giving them details and urging them to scan their own computers.

35. Never participate in chain letters.

Chain letters prey on the weak. There are two main types of chain letter.

The first is an invitation to participate in pyramid selling, where people are encouraged to send money to a list of other people and to join the list themselves so that people lower down the pyramid will send money to them. These schemes are unsustainable. Money does not magically appear out of thin air; the few people at the start of the scheme make money by conning everyone else. Some schemes sidestep the legal issues concerning pyramid selling (which has been made illegal in many countries) by getting the participants to claim that they are selling a low-value product or service, such as a photocopied piece of paper – you should still avoid such schemes.

The second type of chain letter is sent just to cause trouble, rather than to make the originator money. This type of chain letter will typically say things like 'Bob Widget failed to send this letter to ten other people and died the next week.' There are also lots of fake virus warning emails that do the rounds (see #34). This is all total bunkum! Simply delete any emails that you receive if their sole aim is to get you to send on the email to lots of other people. A common tactic is to claim that someone, or some charity, will earn a small sum of money each time the email is forwarded – this is never true, because plain-text* emails cannot be tracked in this way.

See also the section on **phishing** in Chapter 11.

Jokes

36. **Do not forward jokes or other incidental emails indiscriminately to your friends.**

A common complaint that experienced Internet users have is that lots of well-intentioned people forward them the same jokes, funny pictures, etc. If you know the person really well, share the same sense of humour, and know for certain that they appreciate your sending them humorous material, then feel free to send them such things. My recommendation is never to send humorous attachments – the risk of spreading viruses generally outweighs the brief moment of humour that such things might bestow.

Be aware that not everyone welcomes this material. Don't take it personally if someone asks you politely to stop sending jokes. By the same token, don't baulk about telling someone else that you don't appreciate the things that he or she keeps emailing to you: perhaps you have a different sense of humour, or you have usually already seen the jokes.

---

* It might be possible for HTML emails to achieve this tracking if they include images that are fetched from the Web each time the message is opened, but I am not aware of any legitimate instance of this ever having been done in order to pay someone for forwarding emails. Treat any such claims with very high scepticism.

Distribution lists

37. **Don't email lots of people using raw names in the 'To' box. Instead, use a distribution list or BCC.**

   If you need to send the same message to many people, particularly if those people do not all know each other, do not simply include all their email addresses in the TO field. If you do, everyone will be able to see everyone else's email address. There are several reasons why people might want to exercise some control over the distribution of their email addresses, for example if they use different email addresses for different purposes or if they wish to minimise the amount of spam they receive. You should be sensitive to such concerns and use a more appropriate method of distribution.

Spammers are using ever more ingenious techniques to gather 'live' email addresses. Many users' PCs are infected, without their knowledge, by so-called Trojan horse software (see page 103). Some of this software is designed to gather email addresses and to send them to spammers. Therefore, simply by emailing someone whose computer is infected, you may find yourself added to a spammer's list. If someone sends an email to you and a hundred other people, with everyone's email address in plain view, there is a good chance that one or more of the receiving computers will be infected, which could compromise the whole list.

If you receive an email that has been sent to you and other recipients whom you don't know, with all the email addresses displayed, it is bad netiquette to make use of that information. For example, if you offer a product or service, even if you are sure that some people on the list will be interested in it, you should not email them all with details – this would be a blatant spam.

Attachments

38. **Send your emails in plain text unless you need to use formatting to benefit your recipients.**

    The first emails were always plain text. People could still impose a level of formatting by enclosing text within a pair of asterisks to emphasise it (for example, 'are you *really* sure?'), or between underscore characters to represent italics or underlining. Email is still a plain-text system – formatted emails are sent as attachments (usually HTML) to plain-text emails, and most email software displays them automatically.

    There are many benefits to sending and receiving plain-text emails. The emails are smaller, and so are less wasteful of resources. Recipients can choose the font they wish to use to read their messages, rather than having the stylistic preferences of the sender imposed upon them. Plain-text emails without attachments cannot carry viruses.

    While you may like to read your emails in 14-point blue Comic Sans font, it is not wise to impose your tastes on other people. Any formatting whatever will distract the reader from the content of your message, particularly if it makes it difficult for them to read it. Any such formatting in business comes across as unprofessional; embedding fancy graphics, such as the company logo, in each email looks wasteful.

    There are, however, some situations when formatted emails can have a positive benefit to the recipients. For example, many businesses choose to send their customers emails containing details of special offers; by using HTML, they can include pictures of the products, instead of having to direct their customers to their website. Similarly, newsletters that are sent by email may benefit from this formatting. Both of these examples use formatting to improve the service to the recipient. In contrast, most simple emails can (and should) do without any imposed formatting.

39. **Don't send attachments at all unless you need to.**

If you have information to send that happens to be currently in a file such as a word-processed document or a presentation, consider whether it would be more convenient for the recipients if you were to copy the content and paste it into the text of your email.

40. **If you need to send people a large file (say a megabyte* or more), contact them first to check how and when they would like to receive it. Don't just send it as an attachment to an email.**

Remember that not everyone has a broadband connection. Similarly, some people may have a quota restricting the size of email that they can receive, or may pay for their Internet access according to how much data they download.

For very large files, it may be more efficient to upload them to a website or **FTP** server and to restrict your email to instructions about how to access the files. There are also some websites, called **one-click hosters**, that are happy to act as intermediaries for large files.

FTP stands for File Transfer Protocol. See page 82 for netiquette guidelines concerning this protocol.

A **one-click hoster** is a website to which you can upload a large file. You can then email a link to this file to someone else, who can download it from the site.

---

* (Hambridge & Intel, 1995) recommends 50 KB, and (Kallos, 2004) recommends 200 KB, as the definition of a large file. Expect the reasonable threshold to continue to drift upwards over the years – the trend has always been for people to get used to handling larger and larger files.

41. If you are sending photos, reduce their dimensions.

For example, if you take a photo with a digital camera and decide to send it to your friends, resize it so that it is, say, 600 pixels wide. Not

> A **pixel** is a **picture element** – one coloured dot in the photo. A group of one million pixels is called a **megapixel**.

only will this reduce the number of bytes it takes to transmit and store your email, but it will make the image the right size for the recipients to view on their computer screens. Of course, if you are a professional designer emailing some artwork to a client, this rule does not apply!

Image sizes

Digital photos are made up of a grid of coloured dots. A computer monitor may typically be set up with a display size of 1280×1024 pixels, or 1.3 megapixels. By contrast, a good digital camera will use perhaps 8 megapixels for each photo it takes. These extra pixels may be important if you plan to print the photo, but probably aren't useful when viewing it on screen; the recipient of an emailed photo will either have to scroll around the image a screenful at a time to see all the detail, or, more likely, to shrink the photo to fit the monitor, in which case you might as well have resized it before you sent it.

42. Compress files before you send them to someone else over the Internet.

I could have said 'large files', but the same benefit applies even to quite modest-sized files.

The most popular compression scheme at present is the zip format. You can be quite confident that a user you send a zipped file to will be able to unzip it again to restore the original uncompressed files. Other formats may provide a greater level of compression, but it would be polite to check that the recipient is able to handle the format you choose before you send your file. If you are sending graphics files that are already compressed in some way (for example, most jpeg graphics), you won't gain much saving by compressing them further, so just send them as they are.

Privacy

43. **Do not read other people's private emails**

    You might have the opportunity to read other people's emails because you are an administrator, they leave their computer unattended, or there is an email that someone has printed but not yet collected. It is bad netiquette to read other people's emails without their permission – after all, you probably wouldn't like it if they did the same to you.

    The exception to this is where an administrator might have to read users' emails in order to enforce an organisation's email policy. If so, users should be frequently reminded that such checks take place, and emails should be inspected where there is a genuine cause for concern rather than from general nosiness.

44. **Don't use features of your email client that will notify you when someone receives or opens an email that you have sent.**

    For a start, this mechanism isn't guaranteed to work – users can opt not to send these responses, or may be using an email client that doesn't support them anyway. But, more than that, you are disrespecting the recipients' privacy – if they wanted you to know that they had read your email, they could easily reply to it themselves.

Of course, there are some situations, particularly in business, in which such a notification mechanism can simplify the work-flow of a process and improve productivity (for example, if it eliminates the need for follow-up telephone calls to check that important emails have arrived). This rule, in common with all the others, should be taken with a large pinch of common sense.

Related topics

When you think of email netiquette, probably one of the first subjects to come to mind is spam. This is a big topic, and is covered in detail in Chapter 10.

The use of fake emails in order to find out people's passwords as a way to steal money – a fraud known as **phishing** – is discussed in Chapter 11.

3. Forums

Introduction

This chapter gives guidance on the various forms of asynchronous group discussion. It is typical for many people to add to the conversation over time, and for all the messages to be archived somewhere so that they can be searched later. This chapter covers mailing lists and newsgroups. Many of the earlier rules apply here too, but have not been repeated.

Mailing lists

A mailing list is a service where someone can post a message and have it emailed to all the people who have chosen to subscribe. Some mailing lists are one-way – for example, a company may choose to send emails to its customers using a mailing list, but would not normally allow the customers to send messages to the list. In general, this chapter discusses two-way mailing lists, where anyone subscribed to the list may post messages.

Before you start

45. **Lurk before you leap!**

   When you join a new forum, spend some time **lurking**. (Hambridge & Intel, 1995) suggests between one and two months as a suitable time for lurking, although this seems on the long side to me; use however long you think you need to gain an appreciation of the content and tone of the messages that are posted there. After this, don't be afraid to join in – remember that the Internet is for everyone!

> **Lurking** means reading the messages that other people post without contributing to the discussion yourself.

Mailing-list services

Although it is possible to set up mailing-list software on an internet server and run the list independently, many mailing lists are operated via third-party mailing-list services. These are typically free, supported by advertising either inserted into the messages or on the website associated with the mailing list.

At the time of writing, these were the most popular mailing-list services:

- Yahoo! Groups <http://groups.yahoo.com>

- MSN Groups <http://groups.msn.com>

- Google Groups <http://groups.google.com> (Google mix their own mailing lists with archived Usenet discussions).

Posting new messages

46. **Keep your postings on-topic if possible.**

Online forums bring together a wide range of people with an interest in a particular subject. Sometimes you might need some information that is not related to the subject for which the forum was set up, but which you think one or more members of the forum will be able to help you with. Posting such a request would be off-topic for the forum.

Before posting an off-topic message, check to see if there is some other forum that would be more appropriate. If you expect a lot of people to respond to your off-topic post, consider asking people to email you privately and then posting a summary to the list, rather than encouraging a wave of off-topic postings.

47. **If you need to discuss two or more separate topics, post a separate message for each.**

    Different people may be interested in the content of different messages. Separating out the subjects will make everyone's lives easier, especially if a long thread develops about each subject.

48. **If you post a disproportionately long message, indicate this in the subject line, for example by appending '[long]'.**

    Remember that people use email software in different ways. Some people download all their messages to their local computer and then

    > ISP is short for **Internet Service Provider**, the company that provides you with your connection to the Internet.

    scroll through each message in turn; others just look at the subject lines before deciding which messages to read. Some people might even delete certain messages from their **ISP's** server without downloading them. If you have written a long message, it is polite to indicate this in the subject line – people are then free to handle it as they choose, but at least they won't get a nasty surprise if they do choose to download and open it. (Hambridge & Intel, 1995) gives a guideline that anything over 100 lines is considered long.

49. **If you post a message that gives away the ending of a film, book, etc. then clearly mark it as a spoiler in the subject line.**

    > Any information that reveals a plot twist that could spoil someone's enjoyment of a book or film they have not yet seen is called a **spoiler**.

    Not everyone will have seen the film or read the book. People who don't want to know the ending will be able to ignore your message. Of course, if you can word your message in such a way that it doesn't explicitly give the ending away, so much the better.

50.   **Don't post private messages in public forums.**

For example, don't post a message with a subject 'For John Smith only' to a public forum. It might be acceptable to post a message asking John Smith to contact you privately if you know that he is a member of the forum and you have no other way of getting in touch, but consider the wasted resources of your message being stored in many (perhaps many thousands) of copies across the Internet!

51.   **If you send a private message to a mailing list by mistake, apologise to both the intended recipient and the list.**

An apology sent to a forum when you have done something wrong is always a good idea – this is polite, and can help to clear up any confusion about what your message was about. You should apologise to the intended recipient privately, whether or not they are a member of the mailing list to which you sent the message, because your public reply with private information might have caused them embarrassment.

There are two main reasons why people may wish to send a test message to a mailing list: when previous messages that they have sent have not appeared, or when they have received no messages for some time.

52.   **Do not send a test message to a mailing list.**

There are several things you should try before sending a test message to a mailing list. Check that messages are not being blocked by a firewall at your end of the network. Use the management server (typically either a **majordomo/listserv** email responder or a web-based interface) and check that you have not been unsubscribed (as might happen if several messages sent to you bounced for whatever reason). Contact the administrator in preference to sending a 'test – please ignore' type of message to the mailing list.

53. Thank the individual, not the forum.

After you have posted a question or problem to forum, and a solution has been provided, it is polite to give your thanks; however, you should usually do this by sending a private email to the people involved rather than by posting a follow-up message. Although other people might think you ungrateful, you will be saving precious network resources. If, however, you can impart extra information along with your thanks – for example, which of the proposed solutions to your problem worked and which didn't – then feel free to post, since you will be helping other people with the same problem, now or in the future, lifting your response above the 'me too' level.

Of course, if you are a member of a forum where messages of thanks are posted frequently without complaint, you should probably follow suit in order to protect your reputation.

54. If you post a question and get no response, try some other approach.

If at first you don't succeed, give up! Don't post a second message complaining that nobody has responded to your first one and asking the same question again. You might be lucky and get a response this time, but you are certain to annoy people in the process – if people didn't have the answer you needed or the time to respond when you originally asked the question, they probably won't have if you ask it again. You will also be adding red herrings to the results found by people later searching for the same answer. There are many ways of finding out information on the Internet, so switch to one of the others.

Posting replies

The rules for replying to emails in general (see page 23) also apply here, but there are some additional things to be aware of.

55. **In contrast to emails, where new material should be at the top, your response should come below the relevant part of the message to which you are replying.**

    The discussion is easier to read if each point is listed in chronological order down the page.

    > Adding new material before quoted text is called **top posting**, and is frowned upon, particularly on Usenet.

56. **Provide an attribution (such as 'On 3 July 2006 Bob Widget wrote:') before any material you quote.**

    This is a courtesy to both the author of the text you are quoting and the people who will read your message, so they know exactly who said what. Most software will do this automatically.

57. **Read the whole thread (so far) before posting a reply.**

    Don't post a reply just because a suitable comment has popped into your head. Make sure that nobody else has already made the same point. If you haven't got the time to read the whole thread, you haven't got the time to post a response either.

58. **Don't reply to someone's opinion simply to agree with them (no 'me too' messages).**

    Suppose someone writes a message to a mailing list, stating that they think the price of widgets is too high. Perhaps you agree with them – widgets are far too expensive these days. But think before you post a reply saying 'me too'. What information are you actually adding to the discussion? What would happen if everyone who agreed with the original statement were to do the same? Everyone's email inbox would be clogged up with 'and me's and 'me too's instead of coherent discussion about the virtues of Brand X Super Saver widgets and the reasons behind the sharp downturn in global widget production.

If you are thinking about posting a message that is likely to result in lots of 'me too' or 'I disagree' messages, consider using a web-based poll instead. In this way, people can log on to a website to cast their votes, without clogging up the mailing list. After everyone has had an opportunity to vote, you can post a message to the list containing the results of the poll. Some of the websites related to mailing lists (such as **http://groups.yahoo.com**) allow you to create polls; otherwise, there are plenty of websites that will host polls for free.

59. When replying to a message, reply to the mailing list, not the individual.

This rule ensures that all the information about a subject is kept in one place. This can be particularly useful when people come to search for the topic later. Of course, if you need to include private information or you know that your reply will not be of general interest for whatever reason, you should go ahead and reply privately to the author of the message.

60. Keep your posting frequency for replies roughly in sync with that of the other members of the mailing list.

Suppose you subscribe to a mailing list in which most people respond within a couple of hours of the original message being posted. Although it may be more convenient to you to read through the messages once a week and post all your comments in one batch, this is not necessarily convenient for others. You may find yourself resurrecting dead threads (because they are fresh to you), and you may come across as pushy if you appear to be posting many times in a short time (even if the number of responses you send is no greater than other users send over a longer period). See also #110.

61. **Once a thread has run its course, avoid reopening it unless you are genuinely adding useful and relevant information to it.**

If the members of a mailing list need to discuss a single topic for an extended period of time, the discussion is likely to deteriorate into a flame war (see page 111). Most discussions will run their course over a fairly limited time, and it is unhelpful to reopen old topics after the original contributors are likely to have forgotten all about it.

However, sometimes a thread clearly terminates before all the issues are discussed. A good example of this is on support forums where someone asks a question that nobody is willing or able to answer at the time. If a solution is ultimately discovered, it is helpful if someone (ideally the author of the original message) can post this information in a reply, however long has elapsed since the last message in the thread. Such a message is not designed to kick-start the conversation again, but instead as a gesture of kindness toward other people in the future searching the archives for help with the same problem, and ought to be of genuine interest to people who read the original message but were unable to help.

62. **Do not encourage cheating by giving answers to questions that have clearly been set as homework for a course.**

Some people, especially children, see the Internet as a magical oracle that can answer any question. To some extent, they are right. However, homework questions are designed to test the knowledge and skills of the students, and it does them no long-term benefit to have easy access to the answers without having to do any thinking themselves.

A better approach, if you wish to help, would be to point students at sources of information on the Internet or elsewhere that will allow them properly to research the questions they have been set.

Digests

Many mailing lists offer subscribers the option of receiving each message as a separate email at the time it is posted, or a daily digest. In a digest, all the day's messages are included one after the other in a single email (or perhaps several emails, if the list has been particularly busy) sent at the end of the day. This section lists a few rules relating to digests.

63. **Don't quote the whole digest when replying.**

    This is a waste of resources for the recipients of your message, in terms of both the extra unnecessary storage space and the time that they might waste scrolling through the message. See also #25.

64. **When replying to a digest, change the subject line to match the specific message you are responding to.**

    People who choose to receive all the messages as individual emails will generally pick and choose what they read – they probably don't read every single message. If you are replying to a message with the subject 'Good manners' in the 'Uncommonly good etiquette' mailing list, you should ensure that your subject line is 'Re: Good manners' instead of 'Re: Uncommonly good etiquette Digest, Volume 99, Issue 123'. This might still cause problems with threading, as already discussed in #22, but is better than nothing.

65. **Don't ask people to reply off-list just because you are a digest subscriber.**

   If you subscribe to a digest, that is your choice. If you regularly need to receive more timely responses to your messages, you should subscribe to the normal list instead, where every message is sent to you individually as it is posted. If you occasionally need a timely response, consider using the web interface to the list to read the latest messages.

   It is not good netiquette to ask people to change their working practices to fit in with the way you have chosen to use the Internet. Mailing-list messages should be kept on the list so that the discussion is not lost, unless it is an off-topic discussion (see #46).

Unsubscribing

Every so often when you are subscribed to a mailing list, you will see messages posted that are 'unsubscribe' requests.

66. **Do not post a message to a mailing list asking to be unsubscribed.**

   Most mailing lists have a specific procedure that you should go through if you wish to unsubscribe. Typically this is either an alternative address to which you must email your request (e.g. a **listserv** or **majordomo** service) or a website you must visit. You should have received full instructions when you signed up; alternatively, there may be guidance embedded in each of the emails you have received from the list.

The following figure illustrates the raw headers for a mailing-list message. The lines relevant to unsubscribing have been highlighted.

```
Return-Path: <owner-somelist@example.com>
Received: from somewhere.net by mailstore
    for your_address@example.net id 2GVVEc-3dn001-07-EXP;
    Thu, 05 Oct 2006 15:33:04 +0000
X-MimeOLE: Produced By Microsoft Exchange V6.5
Content-class: urn:content-classes:message
MIME-Version: 1.0
Subject: Oops, I was trying to unsubscribe
Date: Thu, 5 Oct 2006 15:51:20 +0100
Message-ID: <B8093E5AF7E2B44C80DD742A85765EF03F04D2@example.org>
Thread-Topic: somelist: Oops, I was trying to unsubscribe
Thread-Index: AcdojexVPoIzrBZLTi3iHXMLhRDWAwABVerQ
From: "Bob Widget" <bob.widget@example.org>
To: <somelist@example.com>
Content-Transfer-Encoding: 8bit
Content-Type: text/plain;charset="iso-8859-1"
Sender: owner-somelist@example.com
Reply-To: somelist@example.com
List-Id: "Just Some List" <somelist.example.com>
List-Unsubscribe: (Use this command to get off the list)
    <mailto: majordomo@example.com?body=unsubscribe%20somelist%20You
r-Email-Address>
Precedence: bulk
```

Many email clients will interpret these headers automatically, and provide you with a menu option for unsubscribing from the list. Otherwise, Bob Widget can see that to unsubscribe he must send an email to **majordomo@example.com**, the body of which must contain the command **unsubscribe somelist bob.widget@example.org** (%20 is the same as a space).

67. Don't let your inbox overflow when you go on holiday.

You don't want your inbox to fill up and start to 'bounce' incoming messages. If these bounced messages are actually posted as messages to your mailing lists, you'll be very red-faced when you come back from holiday (and I don't just mean the sunburn).

You could unsubscribe from the mailing lists temporarily, although most provide some way of temporarily opting out of receiving emails. Another alternative would be to subscribe to the digest form of the mailing list. You may be able to catch up with the messages you have missed by reading them on the Web upon your return.

If you need to resubscribe to a mailing list, don't ask the list administrator to do this for you! There will be a way to do this for yourself (probably very similar to the way you unsubscribed – read the **FAQs** for your mailing list and see #66).

Newsgroups

Usenet (also called **Network News**) has been around for a long time – the first experiments were conducted in 1979. Whereas mailing lists are typically operated

> The term **newsgroup** is used as an abbreviation for **Usenet newsgroup** throughout this book.

from a single server computer that receives the messages and sends them out to the lists' subscribers, Usenet is a network of servers. There are many thousands of **newsgroups**, and the administrator of each server (typically an ISP) must decide which newsgroups to carry. Each server will hold all the recent messages for the newsgroups that it carries, and will allow users connecting to it to read the messages and to post their own messages, which it will distribute to the other news servers on the Internet.

If you don't already have software for browsing Usenet, you could download one of the programs listed at (Open Directory Project, 2006). The best way to start is to read the messages that have been posted to **news.announce. newusers**, which will give you a gentle introduction. If you wish to try sending a message, post it to **misc.test** – you can check that everything works before you start contributing to 'real' newsgroups.

Most of the preceding rules relating to mailing lists are also applicable to Usenet. This section gives raises some additional points that are specific to Usenet.

Message content

68. **Before asking a question, check to see if a similar question has been answered before.**

Check the FAQs to make sure you are not posting a frequently asked question. You can search Usenet with Google Groups at **http://groups.google.**

> **FAQ** stands for frequently asked question. Most forums maintain a list of these. See #68.

com, and a list of FAQs is maintained at **http://www.faqs.org**. Most modern mailing lists have an associated website that you can use to search the archives.

69. **Don't post announcements about major news events to newsgroups.**

As stated in (Horton, Spafford, & Moraes, 1998), by the time most people read newsgroup messages about a major news event, they will long since have been informed by the conventional media. The one exception is the **misc.headlines** newsgroup, which exists for discussing such things.

In contrast, Internet Relay Chat (see page 59) has been used by as a form of communication to get around media blackouts in some major world events, such as the Soviet coup attempt in 1991 and the Northridge earthquake in Los Angeles in 1994. These logs have been archived at (ibiblio, 1999).

70. **Do not post any form of attachment to a newsgroup that doesn't have 'binaries' in the name.**

    Most newsgroups do not welcome binary postings (messages with non-text attachments, such as pictures, videos or software programs) – remember that many newsgroups are high-traffic, and not everyone accessing them will have a fast Internet connection. A related point is that you should post your messages only as plain text, not as HTML or using any other formatting (see also #38).

    Newsgroups that welcome binary postings have 'binaries' as part of the name. An example is **alt.binaries.pictures.animals**, where people send photographs of wildlife.

Cross-posting

71. **Do not cross-post any message to more than 10 newsgroups.**

    This is given as a guideline figure in (Skirvin, 2004). Even this number of newsgroups is probably excessive for most uses, where one or two newsgroups are probably sufficient. You should post to the most specific newsgroup you can find – for example, if you have a question about growing fruit, **rec.gardens.edible** is more appropriate than **rec.gardens**.

72. **Use proper cross-posting instead of sending a separate message to each newsgroup.**

    If you need to cross-post, use the features of your newsreader to send a single message to all the relevant newsgroups at once, typically with a single **FOLLOWUP-TO** header set. In this way the network traffic between news servers is minimised (only one copy of your message needs to be transferred between sites, and follow-up discussions will be confined to the single newsgroup you specified) and smart newsreaders will display your message only once to those people who happen to be subscribed to more than one of the newsgroups you cross-posted to.

73. **Do not post the same message too often.**

Again, where a cyclic posting is necessary (such as for a newsgroup's FAQs), (Skirvin, 2004) recommends posting no more frequently than once every two weeks.

Address munging

74. **If you feel that you must invalidate your email address in some way, so as to avoid receiving spam, make sure that the resulting email address is not valid for some other domain.**

Suppose your real email address is **myaddress@example. com**. Do not use a completely random email address; for example, if you use **dxfj@sdlfkjsfopiu.com** and the domain name **sdlfkjsfopiu.com** exists (or is subsequently registered), you could be contributing to that person's spam burden.

Similarly, you can get software to run on your website which will generate random email addresses. Although

In computing, to **mung** (or **munge**) something means to corrupt it irrevocably. When applied to an email address, this usually means that it cannot be deciphered by software, only by humans. For example, **myDELETETHISaddress@ANDTHIS.example.com** is a munged version of **myaddress@example.com**.

A spambot is a piece of software that explores the World Wide Web looking for email addresses for a spammer to use.

people running such software are trying to combat the problem of spam by filling spammers' databases with invalid email addresses, the possible side-effects are the same as for fake sender addresses.

Some people and organisations that own their own domain names use a 'catch-all' approach, where emails sent to unknown addresses at that domain will be delivered to someone (an individual, or the organisation's administrator). In these cases, randomly generated email addresses are particularly problematic and time-consuming.

If you need to construct an invalid domain name, use the domain-name extension **.invalid**, which has been specifically set aside for this purpose (Eastlake & Panitz, 1999): for example, **fake@email.invalid**. The domain names **example.com**, **example.net** and **example.org** have also been reserved for use in examples, but you should not use these if they are likely to result in traffic to those domains (for example, as part of an email address that might attract traffic).

If you need more information about address munging, see (Baseley, 1999). Although this document was last modified in 1999, it is still being posted occasionally to Usenet and does contain some useful advice.

Additional headers

A message's headers contain all the information about the message – who sent it and when, and which newsgroups it was posted to. These headers are mandatory, but there are some additional headers that are optional, and the correct use of these optional headers has a bearing on netiquette.

75. **Set expiry dates where appropriate.**

When you are posting a message with a limited 'shelf life', use your newsreader software to add an **Expires:** header to your message. This will affect its lifespan on Usenet news servers (reducing the burden on the infrastructure) but not on archives such as Google Groups (so people will still be able to search for your message for research).

76. Allow your messages to be archived.

Google Groups, the largest Usenet archive, supports the **X-No-archive: yes** header. Messages with this header set will not be stored in Google's archive, so will show up in search results for only seven days. Setting this header for all your messages will leave holes in the conversation threads, and will provide no protection against other people quoting some or all of your messages in their replies.

If you are tempted to add this header to the occasional (perhaps controversial) message you send, consider carefully whether you should be posting the message to a public forum such as Usenet in the first place.

Asking for help

Procedure to go through

i. Read the FAQs. You can find a large archive of these at **www.faqs.org**, although they are generally posted regularly to the relevant group.
ii. Search the archives. You can search Usenet by going to **http://groups.google.com**. Other discussion groups will generally have a web-based search facility too.
iii. If your question still hasn't been answered, now is the time to post it to the group. Make sure that you include all the information that people will need in order to answer you – be clear and specific. Explain what you have already done to try to find the answer for yourself.

For a detailed description of how to get help, see (Agre, 1994). This makes some useful recommendations, such as 'know what your question is' and 'provide some context'.

✤ 4. Real-time messaging ✤

Even before the Internet, people were communicating in **real time** with each other over computer networks. On large UNIX networks, the connected users could communicate with one another using programs such as **talk**. This program split the text screen in half, so that you could see what you had written in the top half, and the responses in the bottom half.

Of course, the Internet has opened up this connectivity to everyone, and many people enjoy text-based

> Something that happens without a delay is said to occur in **real time**.
>
> In **real-time messaging**, each user typically has a window that shows all the messages posted by everyone else, as they are posted. This is in contrast to email communication, where a delay is expected between someone sending a message and other people reading it and responding.

chats with their friends from around the world. Nowadays, all messages appear in a single window, each with the name of the user who said it.

Real-time messaging networks

There are two main types of real-time messaging network: instant messaging (IM) and Internet Relay Chat (IRC).

At present, the most popular competing IM networks are **AIM (AOL Instant Messenger)**, **Windows Live Messenger** (formerly **MSN Messenger**), **Yahoo! Messenger** and **ICQ** (a play on 'I seek you'), although new networks and protocols are being developed all the time.

These networks usually supply dedicated software that restricts users to communicating with only other users on the same network. Some modern real-time messaging software supports more than one of these networks, presenting them all in the same way and allowing users to communicate more widely.

The older **Internet Relay Chat (IRC)** protocol is slightly different, in that people join channels on topics of interest, instead of communicating directly with specific people; it is included here because the netiquette aspects are similar to those for real-time messaging in general.

Instant messaging

Most modern computers have some form of IM client installed; in addition, some large ISPs encourage their users to install their own brand of IM software. Most IM software applications support lists of contacts, so users can see at a glance which of their friends are online and can be notified about changes to their status (for example, if contacts become inactive or mark themselves as busy).

77. **Unlike in email messages, it can be permissible to write real-time messages entirely or mainly in lower case.**

    Most people use instant messaging to chat with close friends, so there is often little structure to what is said or how it is written. You will find that you and your friends automatically end up using a similar style – be it all lower case, txt (see #3) or something else – so just use what comes naturally.

78. **When initiating a chat, check that it is a convenient time for the other person.**

    Although people should set their online status to reflect the fact that they are busy, they won't necessarily bother. Just as you might ask 'Is this a good time' when phoning someone, it is polite to check that the person you have contacted online is free to communicate.

79. **Set your online status to reflect accurately whether you are available for chat, busy or away.**

You might find this difficult if you have several methods by which people may choose to contact you online (e.g. IM client and **VoIP**).

> **VoIP** stands for **Voice over Internet Protocol**, a way of making telephone calls over the Internet – see page 87.

However, it is worth the effort. It's not polite to appear to be available, but then to tell people that you are actually busy after they try to contact you.

See also #84 for how to deal with unexpected interruptions in the middle of your chat.

80. **Don't impose your colour scheme on other people.**

Some IM software allows you to set a font type, size and colour. Make sure that these changes are limited to your computer, so you are not forcing your contacts to put up with your personal preferences. They may have poor eyesight, a different-sized monitor, or just an alternative taste when it comes to colour schemes.

81. **Don't assume that the other person is using the same software.**

Although there are only a few IM protocols and networks (such as .NET Messenger Service and Jabber), there are many different clients. Although it's most likely that people will be using the main client for any particular network (such as Windows Live Messenger on MSN), they might not be. Therefore, don't rely on the special features of your client software: if typing (**P**) on your screen produces a picture of a telephone, for example, don't take it for granted that this will be what appears when you send the message – if the other person is using different software, they might just see the text, or they might get a completely different icon.

82. It is acceptable to use standard IM abbreviations*, but be prepared to explain any that the other person doesn't understand.

IM is all about speed. Most people can't type as quickly as they can talk, so commonly used phrases tend to be shortened into abbreviations (rather like those used in mobile-phone text messaging). Some of these (see Appendix A) are so common that most people understand them; in many cases, it would seem strange to type them in full.

If you are a long-time user of instant messaging, be prepared to explain any of the abbreviations you use when communicating with less experienced users. Most people will pick up these terms very quickly and start using them in their own messaging. Remember that, at some point, you came across all these things for the first time too.

83. Write lots of short messages instead of fewer longer ones.

Instant messaging should be just that – instant. The other people in the conversation will usually be able to see that you are typing something, so do not keep them waiting too long to see what it is. IM is a conversation, so it is polite to give people a chance to respond, rather than simply to deliver them a monologue. If you need to type a long paragraph, consider breaking it up and

---

* Some people refer to these as **acronyms**. Strictly, most of them are **initialisms** (words formed from the first letters of the words in a phrase, such as **BRB** for 'be right back') rather than acronyms (initialisms that are themselves pronounceable words, such as **LOL** for 'laughing out loud'). However, I have used the term **abbreviations** throughout this book, which covers all varieties of shortened words and phrases.

sending each line as you finish it, perhaps with an ellipsis (...) at the end to show that you are still typing.

84. **If you have to leave the keyboard unexpectedly and you are in conversation, let the other person know.**

    Although most IM software will notify your contacts when you are away from your computer, there is a time delay before this information is sent (to prevent you from being marked as away every time you pause for breath). Rather than have the other person typing away when you're not there to read the message, it's polite to let them know that you won't be responding for a while. Typically, you would type **brb** (for **be right back** – see Appendix A) when you leave (although **phone** or **doorbell** may be more instructive). Type **bak** (for **back at keyboard**) or simply **back** to announce your return.

Internet Relay Chat (IRC)

The method of communication known as **Internet Relay Chat** (IRC) has been around since 1988, but is still popular today. With IRC, users join channels about the topics that interest them. Channel names start with a # symbol; for example **#unix** or **#football**. A channel is created when the first person joins it, and is deleted when the last person leaves. Everyone in the same channel can see all the public conversation, so IRC is used for many-to-many communication, whereas other forms of IM are often used for one-to-one chats.

In addition to the following rules, you should be aware of the terms of use of the IRC network you choose to join, and any special expected behaviour within the channels you join on that network.

Example of an IRC conversation

85. You may stay logged in to a channel even if you are ignoring the conversation.

This is common practice, so it is generally accepted as okay. Many people just leave an IRC window open all the time, scrolling away to itself. Some client software supports playing a sound when your **handle** is mentioned, so that other users can get your attention.

> A **handle** is the nickname, such as 'bob123', that is visible to other users instead of a person's real name. The term has been borrowed from citizens' band (CB) radio.

86. Use a unique handle.

The only way to identify users is by their handles, so don't choose one that is likely to be in use by someone else. This may be tricky to accomplish, but do your best; for example, **matXstraw** is more likely to be unique than **matthew**, and will help to avoid confusion.

87. Try to stay on topic.

Unless you know all the other users logged in to the channel, try to limit your discussion to the named topic. If you want to chat privately with someone about the world in general, use a different method of doing so. If you want to talk at length about something else, join (or start) a new channel.

❧ 5. World Wide Web ❧

Web browsing

88. **Do not use a pre-fetching web accelerator.**

Some tools appear to speed up web browsing by pre-fetching pages linked from the current page you are viewing, so that they will be in your browser's **cache** (and therefore can be loaded nearly instantaneously) if you click one of the links. Downloading any

> The term **bandwidth** means the maximum possible transfer speed of data from one place to another. A high-bandwidth connection is rather like a large-bore pipe.
>
> A **cache** is a set of web pages stored on disk.

material from the Internet just on the off-chance that you might want to look at it is wasteful – it may save you some time, but it is stealing **bandwidth** (and therefore money) from the sites you are using and causing extra traffic for your ISP.

89. **Do use your browser's disk and memory caches.**

All modern web browsers have the ability to save recently viewed pages to an area of memory or to an area of disk so that they can be retrieved rapidly if they are needed again. This speeds up things such as using your browser's **Back** button. If you turn these caches off, pages will be fetched from the Internet each time instead of being stored locally, which is wasteful of resources.

90. **Do not use your employer's equipment to access materials not directly related to your work.**

    Some employers may turn a blind eye to their employees surfing the Web in moderation (as long as they do not browse offensive or illegal material), in much the same way as they may allow occasional private telephone calls to be made from office phones. However, the most responsible approach is to limit your use of your office computer to tasks directly related to your job.

91. **Email interesting links to friends manually, not by clicking hyperlinks on websites.**

    Some websites, typically those hosting some sort of media such as videos or online games, include hyperlinks with names such as 'mail this link to a friend' or 'tell a friend about this'. Although many such links are innocuous, they do provide unscrupulous people with an easy way to harvest email addresses to sell to spammers. Play it safe, and write the email yourself if you want to pass on details about a website to someone you know.

Reporting illegal content

If you stumble across illegal content online, you can report it to the Internet Watch Foundation (**http://www.iwf.org.uk**). Its remit is to minimise the availability of potentially illegal internet content, specifically

- images of child abuse hosted anywhere in the world

- criminally obscene content hosted in the UK

- incitement to racial hatred content hosted in the UK.

See page 106 for information about reporting phishing scams.

Creating websites

This section provides some guidelines for people who create their own websites. If you don't plan to do this, you can safely skip to the next chapter.

Files

92. **Remember your obligations under international copyright laws.**

This is less netiquette and more a matter of fact. You are not allowed simply to steal content from somewhere else to use on your website. You may be able to quote parts of a larger work if you are discussing it critically, but in general your best course of action is to contact the copyright holder to ask for permission to use their work.

93. **If you make files available for download, check them for viruses.**

Although the users who download the files from your website should also check them, you should take the initiative and check the files to the best of your ability. It would be very bad publicity if you were found to be distributing infected files.

94. **If your website contains adult themes, add metatags to rate the content.**

A **metatag** is an HTML tag that holds information about a web page.

Although most websites want to attract as many visitors as possible, you have a duty to protect sensitive or vulnerable visitors from viewing any content that could cause them offense. This is particularly important in the case of children using the Internet unsupervised.

There are various schemes for voluntarily flagging up adult content. The best known of these is the Internet Content Rating Association's rating system (see **http://www.icra.org**).

Linking

95. **You do not need permission to link to another web page or website; however, you must not misrepresent the target site when you link.**

As stated in (Berners-Lee, 1997), 'The ability to refer to a document (or a person or any thing[sic] else) is in general a fundamental right of free speech to the same extent that speech is free. Making the reference with a hypertext link is more efficient but changes nothing else.'

The reality is a little more complicated than this. There have been various legal cases brought by the owners of websites who felt that other sites were linking to their material in inappropriate ways – some of these cases have been won and some have been lost. The web page (Bechtold, 2004) lists many legal cases – it is no longer being updated, but does demonstrate the complexity of this seemingly simple issue. If the site you are linking to asks you to stop linking to it (particularly if your linking is in any way unusual, such as using frames), and you choose not to remove the link, you should seek legal advice.

In any case, you must not misrepresent the target site. For example, you should not imply a relationship between your site and theirs that does not exist. As always, you must not produce libellous material – keep this in mind when linking to sites that you have discussed on your web page or blog.

96. **If you need to use an image or other file on your website, add it to your site rather than embedding the file directly from another website.**

This presupposes that you have permission to use the file. If you embed the file from another site, then when someone views your webpage the file will be loaded from that other site – this might cost them money in extra bandwidth, and will certainly skew any statistics that they use to gauge the popularity of their site. You are also dependent on the other site not moving or changing the file (in fact, if they catch you stealing their bandwidth then they are likely to modify the file you are linking to so that it says something derogatory). Simply by saving a copy of the file to your own web server and using that instead, you bypass both of these problems.

Of course, some sites may specifically welcome this direct linking. For example, the World Wide Web Consortium (W3C) provides icons for web developers to display on their pages to show that they use valid XHTML. The W3C encourages developers to link directly to the images on their own server – the W3C is willing to accept the extra bandwidth expense in return for being able to easily update the icons (and have those changes automatically reflected on all the sites that embed them in their pages), and they also get some data about the popularity of these icons.

97. **Do not make links open in new pages for no reason.**

Unless you are creating a pop-up window and the original page still needs to be visible, why force the creation of a new window? People are able to use the **Back** button if they need to return to a previous window, and they can choose to open links in new windows for themselves, but it is annoying to have this done automatically. If your site is any good, people will return to it voluntarily without you having to keep it open in a browser window. In particular, don't create new windows just to display advertisements – see #131.

A related point is that if you link to anything other than another web page – for example, linking to a PDF document – you should make this obvious near the link.

Accessibility and standards compliance

98. **Don't create a website that will only work with a particular sort of browser or size of window.**

    Back in the early days of the Web, it was common to see statements such as 'Best viewed with Netscape Navigator' in the footers of web pages. Similar notices encouraged browsers to view a site with a specific window size (e.g. in a maximised window with the monitor set to display 1024 × 768 pixels). This is too demanding of modern web surfers. You should make sure that your website works with all the most popular web browsers and window sizes; if it doesn't then you will lose some potential visitors, which is frustrating for both you and them.

99. **If you need to use advanced features, let them degrade gracefully.**

    For example, if you use **JavaScript** to create drop-down menus, you should provide fall-back static text menus for users who do not have JavaScript

    > **JavaScript** is a programming language commonly used to add dynamic content to websites.

    enabled in their browsers. The alternative would be to leave such visitors stranded on the page without a menu.

    In the same way, when specifying fonts, provide a list of similar fonts so that your page will display uniformly for users on a variety of types of computer – many web-page creation applications will provide this for you automatically.

100. Make your web pages accessible to users with disabilities.

In-depth advice about this is given in the Web Accessibility Initiative's *Web Content Accessibility Guidelines* (W3C Web Accessibility Initiative, undated). You may be required to ensure that your site is accessible anyway, depending on where you live, to comply with your country's anti-discrimination laws.

As a side effect of the changes you make, you will open up your website to any other users who choose non-standard ways of accessing your site, such as with text readers and text-based web browsers. You may also make it easier for search engines to index your site, which could help you to attract more visitors.

101. Check that your web pages conform strictly to the appropriate standards for the technologies they use.

Web browsers tend not to be very strict – they usually try to present the content of web pages even if those pages are poorly constructed. Historically, web browsers have added extensions to the underlying languages of the Web, and have handled ill-formed input in different ways. You stand the best chance that your website will look good and function correctly in all the different browsers if you ensure that the pages adhere to the standards laid down by the W3C. You can check the conformance of any website via **http://validator.w3c.org**.

102. Do not automatically resize the browser window.

Internet users should be able to configure their own working environments however they see fit. They should be in control of which browser they use (see #98), which windows are open (#97) and how big they are.

Remember that modern web browsers allow users to open several pages as tabs in a single window, so a page that resizes its window may also affect other pages.

103. **It is perfectly acceptable to present an email address on your website in such a way that it cannot be harvested by spambots.**

There are various techniques you can use to obfuscate (or **mung**) your email address from **spambots** while making it visible to real visitors to your site; for example, using an image instead of text. Take care not to create fake email addresses that may cause other sites to receive your second-hand spam (see #74). However, do make sure that all legitimate users, whatever their combination of computer and web browser and whether or not they choose to view images and allow JavaScript to run, will be able to see your email address.

Search engine optimisation (SEO)

104. **Don't use tactics designed to boost your search engine ranking. artificially This includes, but is not limited to, using fake keywords (including the names of your competitors), gateway pages and dummy articles.**

As a general rule of thumb, most of the tactics that people use in order to increase their ranking with search engines demonstrate poor netiquette – with the exception of adding real, worthwhile material related to the topic of the site. SEO measures are often counter-productive because search engine developers are continually updating their algorithms in order to counter these tactics, and are likely to mark down any sites that are seen to be trying to manipulate their rankings.

105. Do not allow search engines to index pages that normal users have to pay to access.

This practice is, in effect, spamming the search engine – users of the search engines rightly expect to be able to view the results it gives without having to pay a fee.

Web message boards

Web message boards, or bulletin boards, are rather like mailing lists, but everything is controlled by a website instead of via the exchange of emails. The same rules apply.

6. Blogs and wikis

Blogs

Web logs, or **blogs**, are online journals. They are a relatively new phenomenon, and are proving to be very popular, with bloggers writing about any topic you could think of. Companies are now starting to create corporate blogs as a way of communicating with their customers. By their nature, blog entries are written quickly – communicating news as it occurs. This means that they tend to be less carefully considered than web pages, so there are some things you must be aware of.

106. Only create a blog if you really need one.

Many people are tempted to set up a blog because it seems like a fun thing to do, but they then find that they don't actually have much to say. According to David Sifry, founder of the Technorati blog search engine (**http://www.technorati.com**), over 100,000 new blogs are created every day, and 1.3 million new messages are posted (Sifry, 2006).

I think you will agree that cyberspace is a polluted place, and could do without any more 'what I did on my holiday' ramblings.

If you are a true blogger then you are probably already reaching for your keyboard to knock out a quick post defending bloggers' rights to ramble on about their holidays and whatever else they damned well like. Good for you! The best bloggers tend to be interesting, articulate, perhaps funny, definitely opinionated. Have you got what it takes?

107. Take extreme care if writing a blog about your employer.

Your contract of employment probably restricts some of the things that you are allowed to say about your employer, including not making any of their trade secrets or other commercially sensitive information public. And, of course, you are still bound by various laws; for example, you must not commit libel, whatever the medium.

Whatever grievances you may have against a person, a group of people or an organisation, venting your spleen on the Internet is unlikely to be a productive way of reconciling the situation, and might have legal consequences.

There have been cases of employees being fired for their blogging activities. One example is Ellen Simonetti, who was sacked by Delta Airlines in 2004 after posing in her uniform for pictures she posted to her blog *Diary of a Flight Attendant** (Simonetti, 2006).

The canonical example is that of Heather Armstrong, who writes under the pseudonym Dooce. Armstrong was fired from her job at an unnamed dot-com startup company in 2002 following the satirical postings she made to her blog (Armstrong, 2006). The term **dooced** has since passed into common usage to describe being fired for blogging about one's employer.

108. Cite the source of any information you use in your blog.

Blogs allow you to give your reactions to announcements, events and predictions. If you hear about things from some other source, cite

> A **ping back** is an automatic comment appended to a message when someone links to it from another blog.

it. You would want other bloggers commenting on the things that you have said to do the same. These citations are often supported by blogging systems in the form of **ping backs**.

---

* Now called *Diary of a Fired Flight Attendant*.

However, if you are a new blogger, you have the same right to keep your sources confidential as you would if you were a traditional journalist – see (Electronic Frontier Foundation, undated).

109. Check the spelling and grammar of your blog posts.

Just because it's quick and easy to post a message to your blog, this is no reason to let your standards slip. A blog post will be written once but read many times; spend a little extra time yourself, rather than requiring your readers to trudge through mistakes and spend time working out what you meant rather than what you wrote.

As with emails, avoid non-standard forms of English, such as **txt** and **l33t** (see #3).

110. Post regularly if possible.

Many bloggers post one or more times a day. This is good for their readers, who perhaps look at the blog once a day and so are always guaranteed a fresh posting. If you intend to post less frequently, say once a week, make sure that this information is clear for the casual browser. See also #60.

111. Protect against blog spam.

If your blog allows people to post comments in response to your posts, do what you can to prevent people from using this as a way to post spam. Some unscrupulous people will post links to their own site wherever possible in an attempt to boost its ranking with search engines. This is often automated, with people using software to pump their messages to as many unprotected blogs as they can find. At present, the most common form of protection against this is the **CAPTCHA** (see overleaf), which tries to ensure that only humans can post messages.

It goes without saying (but I won't let that stop me) that you shouldn't abuse the commenting facilities of other people's blogs for blatant advertising purposes. However, if you are adding a genuine response containing a relevant point of view or useful additional information, a link to your website may be appropriate.

Wikis

The most well-known example of a **wiki** is probably **Wikipedia** (**http://en.wikipedia.org**), a web-based collaborative encyclopaedia. Because anyone is allowed to make edits, a wiki can grow very quickly and benefit from the collective wealth of knowledge of its users, but it is also exposed to various forms of abuse (including deliberate vandalism).

A **CAPTCHA*** (Completely Automated Public Turing test to tell Computers and Humans Apart) is a picture of a word or number that has been stretched and skewed in such a way that it is still readable by people, but difficult for software to extract. People must type in the CAPTCHA's text to prove that they are actually people.

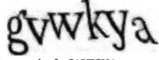

An example of a CAPTCHA.

A **wiki** is a website with pages that anyone can edit online. The word was first used in this context by Ward Cunningham for his **WikiWikiWeb** software, named after the (quick) **Wiki Wiki** bus service at Honolulu International Airport.

112. Do not participate in an edit war.

If two people, or groups of people, disagree about a subject, an **edit war** can ensue, in which the wiki content flip-flops between

---

* CAPTCHA™ is a trademark of Carnegie Mellon University.

This section lists some of the most important RFCs.

== General ==

=== RFC 1855 ''Netiquette Guidelines'' ===

=== RFC 2119 ''Key words for use in RFCs to Indicate Requirement Levels'' ===

This document defines specifically the meaning that should be attached to the following list of key words and
phrases in IETF documents:
* MUST
* MUST NOT
* REQUIRED
* SHALL
* SHALL NOT
* SHOULD
* SHOULD NOT
* RECOMMENDED
* MAY
* OPTIONAL.

== TCP/IP ==

=== RFC 791 ''Internet Protocol'' ===

Summary:

[Save page] [Show preview] [Show changes] Cancel | Editing help (opens in new window)

Please note that all contributions to SWRef may be edited, altered, or removed by other contributors. If you don't want your writing to be edited mercilessly, then
don't submit it here.
You are also promising us that you wrote this yourself, or copied it from a public domain or similar free resource (see Project Copyrights for details); DO NOT
SUBMIT COPYRIGHTED WORK WITHOUT PERMISSION!

Editing a wiki

| article | discussion | edit | history |

Requests for comments (RFCs)

This section lists some of the most important RFCs.

Contents [hide]

1 General
    1.1 RFC 1855 Netiquette Guidelines
    1.2 RFC 2119 Key words for use in RFCs to Indicate Requirement Levels
2 TCP/IP
    2.1 RFC 791 Internet Protocol
    2.2 RFC 793 Transmission Control Protocol
3 Mail
    3.1 RFC 821 Simple Mail Transfer Protocol
    3.2 RFC 822 Standard for ARPA Internet Text Messages
    3.3 RFC 1321 The MD5 Message-Digest Algorithm
    3.4 RFC 2045 Multipurpose Internet Mail Extensions (Part One): Format of Internet Message Bodies
    3.5 RFC 2046 Multipurpose Internet Mail Extensions (MIME) Part Two: Media Types
    3.6 RFC 2047 MIME (Multipurpose Internet Mail Extensions) Part Three: Message Header Extensions for Non-ASCII Text
    3.7 RFC 2048 Multipurpose Internet Mail Extensions (MIME) Part Four: Registration Procedures
    3.8 RFC 2049 Multipurpose Internet Mail Extensions (MIME) Part Five: Conformance Criteria and Examples
    3.9 RFC 2821 Simple Mail Transfer Protocol

The edited page

two different versions of 'the truth' as people edit and counter-edit it. This is not helpful. Ideally, the article should be edited to include both opposing points of view so that readers can come to their own conclusions.

We must learn to be tolerant of other people's edits to our wiki content. If you are not willing to have your carefully crafted prose edited, rewritten, or deleted entirely, do not contribute to a wiki, because you will only be disappointed.

113. Do not use public wikis for marketing or self-promotion.

If you happen to run the authoritative website about a particular subject, do not add a link to it from a public wiki page about that subject; this is unseemly. Sooner or later, if your site is as good as you think, someone else will add the link for you.

Similarly, if you should be famous enough to have an entry in someone else's wiki, resist the temptation to edit it yourself. There have been some high-profile instances of people caught doing this, and it leads to bad publicity.

114. Add keywords as links, even if the target subjects do not yet exist.

Wikis generally allow you to highlight a word or phrase as a link to another topic in the wiki, for example by wrapping it in double square brackets [[like this]] or using capital letters and no spaces LikeThis. If your wiki entry uses plenty of these hyperlinks, it will be easier for people to navigate around the wiki. Links to subjects that don't yet exist are generally welcomed (sooner or later, the missing topic may be created) and such links are usually distinguishable (for example, appearing in a different colour from 'live' links).

See (Wikipedia, 2006, November 28) for Wikipedia guidelines.

PART 2 – ONLINE SERVICES

7. Transferring files

This chapter discusses the netiquette relating to moving files, in particular large files, between computers.

General recommendations

115. Use a download manager.

A **download manager** will allow you to resume your download if your connection is lost part-way through. This means you don't have to start the download again from the beginning, and so is more efficient for both you and the site you are downloading from.

116. Use a local mirror if there is one. Download large files off-peak when possible.

Many popular download sites have **mirror** sites. These hold copies of the main site's content and are spread around the world. Using the mirror nearest to you helps to reduce the demands on the main site and also minimises the amount of intercontinental traffic flowing around the Internet.

Although the Internet is set up in such a way that data will always find a route from its source to its destination, there is a limit to the number of high-bandwidth cables connecting the various hubs of the Internet (for example, cables beneath the Atlantic connecting Europe and the USA). As a result, these particular connections are precious and can form a bottleneck, particularly at busy times.

Bandwidth in general is also important. You are sharing fixed-size 'pipes' with other people, so the more data you pull through, the less is available to them.

It is important to check any files that you download from the Internet to make sure that they do not contain any viruses, spyware, or other forms of malware (see Chapter 11). This is a particular concern when using peer-to-peer download methods (see opposite), because it is less clear where the file originates from.

You will often find that people who create files will supply an official **checksum**, which you can use to check that the file you downloaded exactly matches their original. This is often done using an **MD5 checksum**; the Open Office website gives a good overview of how to use these checksums on different operating systems (Brouwer & Bryan, 2006).

A **checksum** is a short value generated from a larger value. An **MD5 checksum** comprises 16 two-digit hexadecimal (base 16) values (e.g. **069af 81e7dece4cfa8529b17a7c 691ae**) regardless of the size of the original file. If two files generate the same MD5 checksum, it is very likely that they are identical.

FTP

FTP stands for File Transfer Protocol, a technology predating the Web, but still a popular method of transferring files between computers.

Anonymous FTP

117. If an FTP server allows anonymous access, it is polite to use 'anonymous' as the user name and to provide your email address as the password.

This lets the FTP administrators know who has been using the service. If, for example, they discovered that one of their files contained a virus, they could let the people who had downloaded that file know about it. It is unlikely that you will receive spam as a result of supplying your email address in this way to legitimate FTP sites.

Peer-to-peer networks

A **peer-to-peer network** is one in which each computer can connect directly to each other computer without having to go through a central server. One of the first such services on the Internet, and one of the most popular, was Napster.

118. Peer-to-peer networks are not outside the law.

Peer-to-peer networks make it easy for groups of people to share files. Some networks have been accused of facilitating the illegal distribution of copyright material, particularly mp3 music files. Peer-to-peer networks may provide a degree of anonymity, but they still must not be used for illegal activities. If you upload or download copyrighted material without the copyright holder's permission, you are breaking the law!

119. Use a torrent, if available, for large downloads.

If you need to download a large file, say larger than 50 MB, consider using a peer-to-peer download method, such as BitTorrent, in preference to FTP or HTTP download. This

> **BitTorrent** is a protocol for peer-to-peer file transfer, and also the name of the original software application written to support that protocol. The link to a file distributed via BitTorrent is often simply called a **torrent**.

spreads out the network traffic, and allows you to contribute to other people's downloads.

BitTorrent

In a nutshell, BitTorrent works as follows. An initial **seeder** provides a (typically large) file that people might want to download. Other people, called **peers**, connect to the seeder to download the file, but also trade pieces of the downloaded file amongst themselves. This mechanism allows people to share very large files without any one user having to use an excessive amount of bandwidth (as would be the case if all users had to download the file from a single FTP server, for example).

> 120. **After downloading via a torrent, leave your BitTorrent client open until you have shared back at least as much data as you downloaded (i.e. until your share ratio is greater than 1.0).**
>
> You will be sharing some data back as you download the file, so this is not as onerous as it might sound. You are welcome to share data back at a low rate so as not to throttle your own connection to the Internet – it is the quantity of data that you provide, rather than the speed at which you provide it, that is important.

Several high-profile websites relating to BitTorrent have been closed down by the authorities for encouraging the sharing of copyrighted materials without permission. However, BitTorrent has plenty of legitimate uses when transferring large files that are freely distributable and that lots of people want to download, such as distributions of the free Linux operating system.

Note that some BitTorrent clients allow you to view the downloaded parts of certain types of file (such as AVI videos) without having to wait for the whole download to complete. This is one reason why such files are often distributed uncompressed (compression would make the downloads smaller, but they could not be decompressed and viewed until the download had completed).

8. Online auctions

General auction netiquette

121. Do not bid on an item unless you intend to buy it.

The only reason you should bid on an item at auction is that you would be willing to buy it for the amount you bid. Do not bid on items unless you put your money where your mouth is – if you win them, they are yours and you must pay for them.

You may think that this goes without saying, but any seller will tell you that there are a surprising number of timewasters online. Some people bid on high-value items because it makes them feel good, never intending to pay; others bid on several items of the same type and accidentally win more than the one they wanted. Make sure you don't get swept away with bidding fever, finding yourself in one of these categories.

122. Check before you bid that the seller will deliver to your location and will accept a form of payment that you can supply. If you have a question for a seller, ask it before you bid.

Most sellers are happy to answer relevant questions about the items they are selling. What they don't want is retracted bids or non-payment because of misunderstandings. If the seller is unable or unwilling to answer your questions, this is a useful warning against bidding on the item.

123. Leave honest feedback – positive or negative, as appropriate – after each transaction.

Because online auctions are open to everyone, the only mechanism you have for evaluating the risk of buying from or selling to particular members is their feedback score: the number of positive and negative comments left for them as a result of previous transactions. This mechanism is most effective when everyone participates in the scoring.

There have been instances of people buying and selling good feedback. This practice is actively discouraged by the auction sites because it reduces the reliability that honest traders can place on the feedback system and makes life easier for fraudsters.

Sniping

There are two schools of thought regarding **sniping**. The first group maintains that it is a perfectly acceptable thing to do, claiming that it is not an unfair advantage because everyone else is free to do the same thing if they choose. The second group would say that sniping is against the spirit of an auction, and is in some way unfair to both the seller and the other bidders.

Rather than add a rule regarding sniping, I leave it as a matter of individual conscience.

The act of **sniping** is bidding on an auction just before it ends, so that other bidders do not have time to outbid you. Some people use software to place their bids automatically, with only seconds to spare.

The term **sniping** is based on the military practice of shooting at distant targets from cover. This usage, in turn, is believed to derive from **snipe-shooting** – hunting the snipe, a shy and easily spooked species of bird.

❧ 9.   Other online services ❧

Streaming media

124. **When viewing or listening to streaming media (such as online television, video on demand or radio) use the lowest acceptable quality settings.**

     For example, if you only have small speakers then you might not notice much difference between a 32 kb/s streaming download and a 128 kb/s one. In this case, you might as well conserve bandwidth by using the lower quality setting.

VoIP

Voice over Internet Protocol (VoIP) is a relatively new technology that allows real-time spoken communication to take place over the Internet. In effect, any two people with the appropriate combination of hardware and software can talk to each other for as long as they like for free. The netiquette for VoIP is really just common sense, and is much the same as the etiquette governing traditional telephone communication.

125. **Don't call people at random unless they have indicated that they wish to receive such calls.**

     VoIP software, in common with text-based online chat software, allows users to set their status, such as **online**, **busy** or **away**. Although it might be tempting to contact someone at random in a far-flung part of the world just to have a chat, do not do this unless they have set their status to **chat to me** or whatever the equivalent is for the software they are using. Many people use VoIP for business or to keep in touch with a specific circle of friends, and don't welcome random interruptions.

126. Don't use VoIP unless you need an immediate response.

The recipient of a telephone call is interrupted immediately, distracted from what they were doing, and might have difficulty regaining focus afterwards. If you need to contact someone, consider whether it would be more appropriate to use an asynchronous method, such as email, instead.

Domain names

Cyber-squatting

127. Do not register a domain name that a single organisation is likely to want – the name, or a close variant, of the organisation or one of its products – with the intention of trying to sell it to them.

> A **domain name**, such as example.com, is a textual representation of a particular computer on the Internet, typically operated by a single organisation.

Although it is reasonable to register and trade in generic domain names (because there is a fair market for them), cyber-squatting is tantamount to holding a company hostage. You are also likely to have infringed one or more trademarks.

Excessive use of free online services

128. Do not make excessive (typically automated) use of free online services.

This is a bit of a 'woolly' rule, best explained with a few examples of what not to do:

- Do not run a script that checks thousands of domain names each day to see if they happen to have expired.

- Do not misuse a web mail service that supplies a large amount of free storage space by using it as a way of making backups of your documents.

- If you listen to an online radio station, do not leave it streaming 24 hours a day – connect to it only when you are actively listening to it.

PART 3 – OTHER ISSUES

❦ 10.   Advertising and spam ❧

Introduction to spam

Unsolicited commercial messages, known as **spam**, are a big problem on the Internet. They are a particular problem for email users (which means just about everyone), but have also affected Usenet, instant messaging, and other online services.

> The word **spam** means indiscriminate electronic messages, usually emails sent in bulk in order to make money for the sender by advertising a product or service, or encouraging people to buy a particular stock.

This chapter groups together all the netiquette guidelines relating to spam, and also gives some advice about legitimate ways in which companies can advertise their goods and services on the Internet.

The origin of the term spam

The use of the term **spam** on the Internet comes from a Monty Python's Flying Circus sketch, set in a café where almost every item on the menu contains SPAM™ luncheon meat*:

* Egg and bacon

* Egg, sausage and bacon

* Egg and SPAM

* Egg, bacon and SPAM

* Egg, bacon, sausage and SPAM

---

* SPAM™ is a trademark of Hormel Foods, who have been producing luncheon meat under this name (short for 'spiced ham') since 1937. The word 'spam', meaning unsolicited commercial email, should be in lower case to distinguish it from the food.

- SPAM, bacon, sausage and SPAM

- SPAM, egg, SPAM, SPAM, bacon and SPAM

- SPAM, sausage, SPAM, SPAM, SPAM, bacon, SPAM, tomato and SPAM

- SPAM, SPAM, SPAM, egg, and SPAM

- SPAM, SPAM, SPAM, SPAM, SPAM, SPAM, baked beans, SPAM, SPAM, SPAM and SPAM

- Lobster Thermidor aux crevettes with a Mornay sauce served in the Provençale manner with shallots and aubergines, garnished with truffle pâté, brandy and with a fried egg on top and SPAM

The sketch is interspersed with a chorus of Vikings singing repetitively about 'Lovely SPAM! Wonderful SPAM!' Given the way that unwanted emails can litter your inbox, falling between the tasty morsels you actually wish to consume, it's not surprising that **spam** was adopted as a term for these.

Email spam

129. Don't send spam.

It is a sad fact that most of the email that is sent is spam. Most people don't want to receive any spam. The fundamental difference between bulk mail advertising sent via the postal system and spam is the cost. Bulk mail is comparatively expensive to send, but essentially free to receive; spam email is very cheap to send, but causes costs to the recipient (and the other participants in the delivery chain, such as ISPs) in terms of bandwidth and storage, and, perhaps most importantly, the time it takes to delete the unwanted messages. The cheapness to the sender is why it is cost-effective for the largest spammers to send millions of emails each day – they need only the tiniest of response rates to recover their costs. This explains why your email inbox may be full of offers for prescription drugs and extensions to parts of the male anatomy – clearly aimed at the small and vulnerable group of people whose embarrassment at the thought of seeking professional medical advice is great enough that they would rather trust their health to complete strangers. You will never see such offers in an envelope on your doormat – the response rate would not be high enough to justify the postage cost.

If you do send spam, you risk alienating potential customers and being disconnected by your ISP (sending spam is against the terms and conditions laid down by most ISPs). Those people who send spam using a false return address already know that they are acting wrongly – there is little hope that reading pleas such as this one will be sufficient to make them stop wasting other people's time and money.

If you have a product or service to advertise on the Internet, there are many legitimate methods open to you (see page 99). Use one or more of these instead.

If you do have cause to send an unsolicited email to someone, be sure to explain where you got their contact details from. For example, if there are only half a dozen widget retailers in your city, and you are a local manufacturer of widgets with a new product, then stating that you got the contact email addresses by browsing through the National Association of Widgetmongers business directory will give your message more credibility than if it appears that you have just chosen email addresses at random.

130. Don't respond to spam.

If you buy a product or service that has been advertised by spam, you are adding to the profitability of the spammer. This means that Internet users in general, and you in particular, will keep receiving unsolicited commercial emails, as you will have encouraged the spammers to continue with this method of promotion and will have marked yourself out as a good sales lead for future campaigns.

Many spam emails include hyperlinks that claim to allow you to opt out of future mailings. Not all of these are legitimate, and you should not click them. Similarly, replying to a spam email is likely to be ineffectual at best (most use fake return addresses) and might confirm to the spammer that your address is 'live', which will actually cause you to receive more spam (they may well sell your details on to other spammers)!

Perhaps the one exception to this is the automatic anti-spam solution that challenges each new sender by quarantining their email and sending them an email asking them to confirm their identity. Legitimate senders will take the appropriate action (typically replying to the email or visiting a particular web page), thus unlocking their quarantined email and adding them to a whitelist so that all their future emails will be delivered to the recipient; spammers won't bother to respond (or, more likely, will never see the challenge email), so the spam will never reach its intended target. Although such systems generate many challenge emails that will themselves bounce or will reach the inbox of innocent parties whose email addresses have been 'borrowed' by spammers, the aims of these systems are laudable and their use should be encouraged. (But do make sure that you manually add any mailing lists that you join, so as not to inconvenience the administrators with challenge emails.)

Newsgroup spam

Usenet is generally regarded as the birthplace of spam. Although inappropriate email messages can be traced back at least as far as 1978 (Templeton, 2005), it was on Usenet that spam first became a significant problem to a large number of users.

Although there were a few incidents of newsgroup spamming in the early 1990s, these tended to be political rather than commercial, and created by hand. This all changed in 1994 when husband-and-wife Arizona lawyers Laurence Canter and Martha Siegel allegedly paid a programmer, Leigh Benson*, to write a program to post an advertisement to every newsgroup on Usenet:

```
Subject: Green Card Lottery- Final One?
From:  Laurence Canter <nike@indirect.com>
Date:  Tues, Apr 12 1994 8:40 am
Email:   nike@indirect.com (Laurence Canter)
Groups:   alt.brother-jed, alt.pub.coffeehouse.amethyst, etc., etc.

Green Card Lottery 1994 May Be The Last One!
THE DEADLINE HAS BEEN ANNOUNCED.

The Green Card Lottery is a completely legal program giving away a
certain annual allotment of Green Cards to persons born in certain
countries. The lottery program was scheduled to continue on a permanent
basis.  However, recently, Senator Alan J Simpson introduced a bill
into the U. S. Congress which could end any future lotteries. THE 1994
LOTTERY IS SCHEDULED TO TAKE PLACE SOON, BUT IT MAY BE THE VERY LAST
ONE.

PERSONS BORN IN MOST COUNTRIES QUALIFY, MANY FOR FIRST TIME.

The only countries NOT qualifying  are: Mexico; India; P.R. China;
Taiwan, Philippines, North Korea, Canada, United Kingdom (except
Northern Ireland), Jamaica, Domican[sic] Republic, El Salvador and
Vietnam.

Lottery registration will take place soon.  55,000 Green Cards will be
given to those who register correctly.  NO JOB IS REQUIRED.

THERE IS A STRICT JUNE DEADLINE. THE TIME TO START IS NOW!!

For FREE information via Email, send request to
cslaw@indirect.com

--
**************************************************************
Canter & Siegel, Immigration Attorneys
3333 E Camelback Road, Ste 250, Phoenix AZ  85018  USA
cslaw@indirect.com  telephone (602)661-3911  Fax (602) 451-7617
```

---

* An interesting first-hand account of his involvement with Carter and Siegel can be found in (Leavitt, undated).

This message caused an outcry, and popularised the use of the term spam. People also objected to the content of the message – all that someone needed to do to enter the 'green card lottery' was to send his or her name and address on a postcard to the organisers of the draw, so there appeared to be no reason for anyone to pay Canter and Siegel for assistance with this.

Canter was reportedly disbarred in 1998 for numerous violations of the attorney disciplinary rules – although the press release announcing this (available as part of [Leavitt, undated]) doesn't mention spam, an article in *Wired* magazine (Craddock, 1997) quotes William W. Hunt III of the Tennessee Board of Professional Responsibility as saying, 'We disbarred him and gave him a one-year sentence just to emphasise that his email campaign was a particularly egregious offense.'

The moral of the story? Don't spam on Usenet (or anywhere else for that matter).

Organisations committed to reducing spam

Coalition Against Unsolicited Commercial Email (CAUCE)	**www.cauce.org**
Spamhaus	**www.spamhaus.org**
Abuse.net	**http://spam.abuse.net**

Advertising on the Web

131. Never use pop-up or pop-under advertisements.

Nobody welcomes these. People go to great lengths to prevent adverts from opening in new windows in their browsers. If you need to display advertising, do so within the bounds of your content pages.

132. **Do not use graphical adverts that are designed to look as if they are interactive.**

> A graphical user interface (GUI) consists of the windows and icons you use to interact with your computer.

For example, do not include GUI elements such as 'Close' buttons, or animated 'click the moving character' banners. Such adverts are designed to trick people, particularly inexperienced Internet users, into clicking on them. There are plenty of ways of making advertisements enticing without resorting to such trickery.

Legitimate advertising

Email

One way to get your advertising into people's emails without spamming is to take out an advert in an email newsletter on a related topic. Most of these newsletters are free to receive, making their money from selling advertising space, and the recipients either welcome the adverts, or at least understand the need for them. These newsletters are easy to find by searching the Web.

Furthermore, some people actively welcome targeted commercial email, and sign up with companies that will supply them with this information, such as **infobeat.com** and **postmasternetwork.net**. Again, you can find other companies by searching the Web.

Newsgroups

Some mailing lists and newsgroups (particularly **comp.newprod**[†], the ***.announce** newsgroups and the **biz.*** hierarchy) welcome on-topic advertisements. Read the FAQs first; these might specify particular formatting, such as adding **ANN:** to the front of the subject for

---

[†] Although this seems to have fallen out of use.

announcements. You should assume that any group that does not explicitly say it welcomes advertisements does not wish to receive them.

However, few groups object to people giving a small amount of commercial information as part of their **sig** when they post, as long as their posts are relevant. If you are an expert on a subject, posting answers to people's questions in a relevant group is an excellent way of helping others, raising your profile and advertising your website (via your **sig**).

> A **sig** or **signature** is a fixed block of text used to give contact information and added automatically to every email sent. See #4 for information about formatting sigs.

The Web

There are very many ways to advertise on the Web. As noted in the earlier rules, some of these advertisements are still rather intrusive, but I find that Web advertisements in general are still preferable to spam emails.

At present, the largest scheme for advertising on the Web is probably Google AdWords (Google, 2006). A quick search of the Web will find you dozens of others from which to choose. You could, of course, find a website relevant to the product or service you are offering and contact them directly about advertising on the site.

11. Security

If you have a computer that connects, directly or indirectly, to other computers, you have a duty of care to protect that computer in order to reduce the risk to the network as a whole.

Viruses

In this section I have used the term **virus** to mean any form of malware, in order to simplify the discussion. From a user's point of view, the distinction may not be important – most virus checkers also check for other types of malware – but more correct definitions are given below for those who are interested.

The term **malware** refers to any software that deliberately causes harm to computer systems.

A **virus** infects an existing program so that the virus is run whenever that program is run; viruses can replicate. Viruses may cause damage accidentally (as a by-product of infecting the programs) or intentionally (for example, by deleting data on a predetermined date).

A **Trojan horse** is non-replicating malware that typically undermines the security of the computer system, allowing hackers to gain access.

A **worm** is a self-contained application that, when run, attempts to copy itself over a network.

Spyware is software designed to watch users without their consent and report their actions back to some third party – this can be as innocuous as controlling the adverts that they see, or as malicious as stealing their passwords, credit card information, and so on.

---

133. **Make sure you have a virus scanner, keep its virus definition files up to date, and run scans regularly.**

It's no use having an outdated virus scanner that is unable to protect you against the latest threats. This would be like vaccinating your child against smallpox but not against bird flu, or some other current disease.

If your computer contracts a virus, it should be your top priority to hunt it down and wipe it out. Viruses can spread very quickly, and other computer users will be justifiably angry if you pass it on to them.

134. **Enable macro virus protection in your office software suite.**

Make sure that your office software warns you whenever you open a document that contains macros. Macros can contain viruses; if you open a document containing a macro virus, it will infect your other documents. Never allow macros to run unless you trust the source of the document and expect it to contain macros.

135. **Don't open email attachments unless they were sent from someone you know and you were expecting the attached files.**

Many viruses spread by sending emails from an infected PC with an infected file as the attachment. Different viruses will get the list of email addresses that they will try to spread to from a variety of sources, such as the web browser's cache of visited web pages (some of which will contain email addresses) and the email address book of the infected computer. Because of this, you might receive an infected email from someone you know if their computer has been compromised. It is generally better to err on the side of caution – you can always email the sender, to double-check that they really did send you a legitimate email, before opening anything suspicious.

Trojans and spyware

A **Trojan** (or **Trojan horse**) is a program that you think is useful, but which actually poses a security threat. For example, you might download a game from the Internet that actually allows hackers to gain full access to your PC; they can then steal your personal information (such as your credit card details and website passwords) or use your PC to send spam emails to other people without your knowledge. **Spyware** is software that watches what you do and relays that information over the Internet to some third party. The netiquette relating to both these threats is the same.

136. **Make sure that you have a firewall installed that checks both inbound and outbound Internet traffic.**

> A **firewall** is a hardware or software device that applies security rules to prevent certain traffic from passing between networks.

Some firewalls, such as the one supplied with Windows XP*, check only the traffic coming in to your PC. This is still useful to prevent hackers from gaining access directly, but offers little or no protection against Trojans that you inadvertently install yourself.

Make sure that whichever firewall you use asks for your permission before the applications on your PC can send data onto the Internet. This gives

> A **port** is a numbered virtual device via which connections between computers are made.

you an extra level of protection. If an application attempt to send data unexpectedly (for example, a game trying to open a **port** for incoming connections), you can block it and investigate.

---

* The Windows Vista firewall does allow blocking of certain outbound traffic, but this is not turned on by default.

There are many websites that offer to check the security of your PC online. You should use these on a regular basis in addition to installing applications (anti-virus, anti-spyware and firewall) to protect your PC. Note, however, that some Trojans do themselves pose as anti-spyware software; check out the list at (Spyware Warrior, 2006) before downloading anti-spyware software. (Bear in mind that this list is maintained by a commercial supplier of anti-spyware software.)

Phishing and other fraud

137. **If your organisation sends emails to customers, make it a policy never to include hyperlinks to your website's logon pages, and make sure that your customers know this.**

Phishing scams rely on people following the links in emails sent to them. Your organisation and its customers are less likely to suffer loss if a clear policy is in place stating that no legitimate emails will be sent with logon hyperlinks – this makes it harder for the illegitimate phishing emails to appear credible.

> **Phishing** is the illegal practice of setting up clones of real websites to steal usernames and passwords from users. This is typically done by sending fake emails to banking customers.

138. **If you receive a phishing email, forward it with full headers to the organisation that is being targeted.**

Most organisations have a dedicated email address for receiving phishing reports. It is best to report every phishing email you receive – without this information, organisations will not be able to close down the fake websites that are being used fraudulently. Make sure that you include the full headers from the original message, because these may be useful to the person investigating your report.

One can easily imagine that such email addresses receive a very large number of reports; after all, the phishers probably send out several million emails each time. This might put you off sending the report, thinking that someone else will do it for you. Although this is possible, even likely, the affected organisations would rather receive many identical reports than have one fake website slip through the net. In addition, phishers may well be using a pool of fake sites; therefore, even though the text of the email you receive may be identical to one already reported, the site that needs closing down could be different.

139. **Do not send confidential information, such as credit card numbers, by email unless you encrypt it first.**

Normal email is not a secure way to send private information. Think of it as more like sending a postcard than a letter – your email will be sent as plain text and be passed through several computers on its way to your recipient. The owners of those computer systems could, if they so wished, read your message in transit.

Another danger with sending confidential emails is that they will be stored, perhaps for a long time. If you send a company an email with your credit card number, that email will probably be stored in your own outbox and on the company's email system – although you can delete your own copy, you have no control over what the recipient does with it. Given the prevalence of malware, why risk the company getting infected with software that scans their saved emails for credit card details and then emails that information to a fraudster?

If you want a single place to report all the phishing emails you receive, send them to the Anti-Phishing Working Group (http://www.antiphishing.org), which is a global organisation with over 2500 members. Their email address for reports is reportphishing@antiphishing.org. An alternative, community-based phishing repository is PhishTank (http://www.phishtank.com), where suspected phishing emails must be entered on the website instead of being reported via email.

At the time of writing, some of the most popular targets of phishing scams were using the following email addresses to receive reports (they are, of course, subject to change):

- eBay   spoof@ebay.com or use the online form available from the Security & Resolution Center link on the homepage.

- PayPal   spoof@paypal.com

- UK banks   You can report any phishing email targeting UK banks to Bank Safe Online (http://www.banksafeonline.org.uk), using the address reports@banksafeonline.org.uk. In addition, most banks have their own email addresses that you can use for your reports.

Reports of phishing emails targeting customers of banks from other countries, or of any other companies, should be sent to the general clearing houses listed above. Remember to include full headers (see #138).

See page 64 for information about reporting other forms of illegal content via the Internet Watch Foundation.

Common types of email fraud

In an **advance fee fraud**, the fraudster sends out many unsolicited emails offering huge rewards in return for some help. The fraudsters will ask everyone who responds for an administration fee; this is much smaller than the promised amount, but is typically not mentioned in the first email. The fraudsters will encourage people to send this fee, and may repetitively ask for more and more money if they think they can get away with it. Needless to say, the promised large sum of money never materialises. A common type of advance fee fraud is known as **419 fraud** (named after the section of the Nigerian* criminal code relating to it) where someone claims to need foreign assistance to help them to transfer a large sum of money (usually millions of US dollars) out of the country, for which the helper will supposedly get a cut. Again, no money will be forthcoming, and people who respond will be milked for fees and may have their bank accounts emptied for good measure!

Whereas advance fee frauds usually require some interaction by the scammer, **phishing frauds** can largely be automated. Fraudsters can easily contact millions of potential suckers, harvest their account login details, and steal money from them, as if working a giant conveyor belt.

Pyramid schemes are often operated by email. In such a fraud, people join the scheme by paying money to existing members, which then allows them to collect money from new people joining the scheme lower down the pyramid. A little thought shows why this is unsustainable – the scheme needs an ever greater number of suckers to fund the people higher up the pyramid, and no actual value is being created. These schemes have been declared illegal in many countries.

---

* The apparent success of this fraud means that it is now a worldwide problem.

12. Miscellany

Spelling and grammar

Sloppy spelling in a purely written forum sends out the same silent messages that soiled clothing would when addressing an audience. (Templeton, 1999)

140. **Use correct spelling and grammar.**

In terms of etiquette, the main problem with poor spelling and grammar is that you are making it more difficult than it should be for people to understand what you have to say. If you know that your spelling and grammar are not good, take the time to spell-check your work before sending it to other people – it's not fair to waste their time just because you are too lazy to do this.

A common mistake is the use of multiple exclamation marks or question marks for emphasis!! A single question mark is always sufficient at the end of a question (isn't it???). Most of the time, even a single exclamation mark is overkill – the less frequently you use them, the more punch they will have when they do crop up.

141. **Do not post a message just to correct someone else's spelling or grammar mistakes.**

Such a message would be off-topic and could be considered a flame (see page 111). You might consider emailing the person privately if you feel that they are misusing terminology, but do not expect to be thanked for this (you may be thought to be pedantic and cause offence). The same advice goes if you notice errors in a message you posted – if you have more to contribute to the discussion, you may decide to correct your mistake at the same time, but otherwise it's probably not worth a message of its own (unlike factual errors).

URL shortening

142. If you need to include URLs that people are likely to type in, consider providing a shortened version. It is best to provide the full expanded URL as well, unless space in your publication is particularly tight.

> A URL is a **uniform resource locator**: usually a web address such as **http://www.w3.org**.

There are several free websites (for example, **tinyurl.com** and **snipurl.com**) that will provide short URLs that redirect to longer URLs of your choice.

Providing the full version as well gives some insurance against problems with the intermediary website, especially if people come to look at your post in an archive in the future.

Optional payments

The Internet is young, and its various business models are still evolving. Some services are totally free; others charge a subscription or other fee for their use; still more rely on revenue from advertising. Somewhere in the middle are the freely available services that nevertheless rely on user contributions for their continued existence.

143. **If you frequently use an online resource that depends on user contributions, contribute.**

You are benefitting from the contributions of others, so it is only fitting that you do your bit. The benefit of funding services in this way is that users need only contribute what they can afford and what they think the service is worth.

User-supported websites

Here are some notable online resources that are funded by donations from users:

- some online radio stations, such as Radio Paradise (**http://www.radioparadise.com**), which don't have adverts

- various open-source software projects on Source Forge (**http://www.sf.net**)

- the online encyclopaedia Wikipedia (**http://www.wikipedia.com**), which accepts donations to help fund its infrastructure

- many thousands of shareware software applications

Fanning the flames

A disproportionate number of arguments take place online. This is partly because text-only communication strips away many of the nuances (visual and tonal) that help to reinforce the message in face-to-face communication. Another reason is that the Internet is the world's largest social network, where you are sure to find every possible opinion expressed.

A **flame** is an insulting personal comment.

Flamebait is a message posted with the sole intention of causing trouble. A **troll** is someone who posts such messages (**troll** is an angling term for enticing fish by drawing bait through the water).

A **flame war** is an online discussion that has broken down to the extent that it is little more than a series of personal attacks.

In his book, (Belbin, 2003), first published in 1981, R Meredith Belbin determined that people could be categorised into a small number of groups: **Shaper, Finisher, Completer Finisher, Co-ordinator, Teamworker, Resource Investigator, Plant, Monitor Evaluator** and **Specialist.** Historically, the early adopters of the Internet have had a large proportion of Specialists. One of the characteristics of the Specialists is that they don't enjoy having their opinions questioned. When you get two individuals or groups with conflicting views, the discussion can heat up until it eventually turns into a **flame war.**

Perhaps the best way to avoid being sucked into a flame war yourself is to ensure that you do not directly challenge the views of people who consider themselves to be experts. If you do, make sure you can back up your arguments with hard facts!

144. If you need to post something controversial, wrap it between <flame> and </flame> tags.

By highlighting your post in this way, the recipients will know that you are aware of the delicacy of what you have said, and they are likely to be more sympathetic in their responses. This may allow you to get your point across and stimulate discussion rather than initiating a flame war. An alternative style is to write **FLAME ON** at the start and **FLAME OFF** at the end.

145. Do not troll.

Do not participate in forums in which you are likely to find much of the content objectionable. People have a wide variety of interests, and you will find all of these expressed and discussed on the Internet. If you find yourself wanting to join a forum in order to shape other people's ethics or morality to match your own, you are asking for an angry response.

When you start by telling those who disagree with you that they are not merely in error but in sin, how much of a dialog do you expect?

Thomas Sowell (1930–), American economist and commentator

146. **Do not respond to trolls.**

Trolls are out to cause trouble. They want attention and to provoke a reaction. Don't rise to the bait, and they are more likely to wander off to more fertile hunting grounds.

147. **On Usenet, keep discussions about the respective merits of competing technologies to the 'advocacy' newsgroups in the 'comp' hierarchy.**

In general, discussions along the lines of 'my bright shiny kit is better than yours' are likely to deteriorate into flame wars. Quarantine such emotive discussions in the newsgroups set up to hold them.

148. **If you feel that a misunderstanding via email has brought you to the brink of a flame war with someone you know, do not try to use email to resolve the situation. Instead, meet face to face or call them on the telephone.**

This advice is given in (Kallos, 2004), and seems eminently sensible for all the reasons already discussed regarding the impersonal nature of email communications and the loss of tonal context from visual and aural clues. As Kallos says, 'Many times, e-mails will only exasperate an already-sticky situation unless both parties are articulate and deliberate communicators.'

If this doesn't work, a final possibility would be to ask a neutral third party, ideally one who knows the participants in the discussion, to intervene and cool things down. This is more likely to be necessary in a business context than in a general online discussion, particularly if some compromise decision is needed.

149. If you have said or done something wrong, apologise.

Perhaps the simplest way of calming a fraught situation is to apologise for anything you have said or done that you now regret. By doing this, you are renouncing not necessarily the opinions you have expressed, but perhaps the tone in which you have said them. If other parties continue to flame you, this will reflect badly on them; either way, your courage to apologise will be respected by any independent observers in the forum.

Legal considerations

Trademarks

It is a common idiom to use the trademark letters (TM) for comedy effect – for example, 'this is the Next Big Thing (TM)'. Although you are unlikely to be prosecuted for such a transgression, the capitalised words alone are sufficient to indicate that you are using a cliché deliberately.

Laws

As mentioned elsewhere in this book, don't fall into the trap of thinking that the law doesn't apply in the online world. It does. Infringement of copyright is still infringement of copyright; libel is still libel; theft is still theft.

Hardware

Wireless networks

150. Run wireless networking equipment at the lowest power you need.

Some wireless networking equipment allows you to alter the strength of the signal, and, as a result, the effective range of the equipment. If you need only a short range, you should reduce the power of the signal. This makes it less likely that your signal will interfere with other wireless networks in the area, and has the added benefit of reducing the threat of unauthorised people accessing your network. As a side effect, it may also use less electricity.

The environment

The following rules aren't strictly netiquette, but they do relate to general good citizenship and concern computers.

151. Consider the environmental effect of the way you use your computer.

As an example, instead of running a screen saver, it may be better to set the screen to blank after a given period of inactivity. This way, it can power itself off more quickly.

When your computer is not in use, it saves electricity if you turn it off completely instead of leaving it fully on or on standby. You can buy smart power supplies that automatically power down your peripherals when they detect that you have switched off your PC.

152. **Use your computer to reduce the amount of waste paper you produce.**

Many companies now send bills and statements to their customers over the Internet instead of by post. Not only does this reduce the amount of waste paper created, but it saves the company money (which, in turn, may be passed on as savings to the customer).

153. **Dispose of old computer equipment in an environmentally responsible way.**

Most computer equipment, however old, still has a value to someone somewhere. Many charities are happy to receive donations of computer equipment, and even broken computers will be useful to someone for spares.

Protecting your children online

Parents and guardians should make sure that the children in their care understand and comply with the following rule.

154. **Never give out your personal details in online chatrooms.**

This is a very important rule. People you meet online may not be who they say they are. There are plenty of ways to communicate online; do not give out any information, such as an address or telephone number, that would enable other people to find you in 'real life'.

You can find more information about this and related issues on the website of the Internet Watch Foundation (see page 64). In particular, they provide a useful *Safe Surfing Links* page at (Internet Watch Foundation, 2006).

Emoticons

There are hundreds of possible **emoticons** (also called smileys), but you might like to restrict yourself to the following widely understood ones rather than the more elaborate ones that might be misunderstood:

Emoticon	Description
:-) or :)	Smile
:-(or :(	Frown
;-)	Winking smile (usually indicating that you shouldn't take this too seriously)
:-D	Grin

As with exclamation marks and question marks (see #140), if you use only a moderate number of emoticons in your message then each will have more impact that it would if your message were littered with them. They should probably be avoided altogether in business correspondence – remove both the emoticon and the inappropriate material that it is indicating.

Standard administrator email addresses

Most organisations will forward some standard email addresses to particular administrators. For convenience, your organisation should probably use such addresses and redirect them to the appropriate administrators. You might find that you receive additional spam as a result, but it would be polite to take the hit for the benefit of real people trying to contact you. Any spammers stupid enough to send spam to your postmaster address definitely deserve to be tracked down and reported!

The following table lists the most common administrator email addresses.

Address	Example	Description
abuse	abuse@example.com	Where example.com is an ISP, this address is usually the place to send reports about spam emails that have originated from their network. (But be careful, because spammers often forge email headers to prevent detection.)
hostmaster	hostmaster@example.com	The person in charge of the domain name and web server for the organisation.
postmaster	postmaster@example.com	The person in charge of the organisation's email system.
webmaster	webmaster@example.com	The person in charge of the organisation's website.

A more complete list, together with supporting documentation, can be found in (Crocker, 1997).

13. Conclusion

Just as some people eat with their mouths open or talk loudly on their mobile phones in public places, certain people will act on the Internet without regard to the needs and sensibilities of others. Sometimes this is through ignorance – they weren't aware that their actions would negatively affect other people – and sometimes it is a deliberate trampling of other people's time and resources, as in the case of spammers.

The fact that you are reading this book suggests that you are 'one of the good guys'. You care about the impression you give and the impact that your actions have on other people. You probably don't drop litter in the street, but every day you see evidence that some people do. Although you don't swear in the presence of children, you often hear parents doing exactly that. Different people live by different rules – online as well as off. Whereas you can't do much about other people's actions directly, you can set a good example by demonstrating good netiquette yourself and hope that others follow suit.

Bear in mind the following quotation from *In The Sorrows of Young Werther* by Johann Wolfgang von Goethe (1749–1832): 'Misunderstandings and neglect occasion more mischief in the world than even malice and wickedness. At all events, the two latter are of less frequent occurrence.' In other words, 'assume good faith'.

As stated in (Horton, Spafford, & Moraes, 1998), 'It is never a good idea to carry on "meta-discussions" about whether a given discussion is appropriate – such traffic mushrooms until nobody can find articles that belong. If you are unhappy with what some user said, send him/her mail, don't post it.'

Appendix A – Instant-messaging abbreviations

The following list explains the meanings of the most common abbreviations used in instant messaging; they may be in upper case or lower case. Note that some of these expand into expletives, and so should only be used where this is unlikely to cause offense (although, for example, RTFM is commonplace and RTM is rare).

AFAIK	As far as I know...	IC	I see!
AFK	Away from keyboard	ICBW	I could be wrong...
ASL	Age / Sex / Location?	IDK	I don't know!
ATM	...at the moment...	IGMC	I'll get my coat! (Typically used after a bad pun.)
BAK	Back at keyboard		
BFN	Bye for now	IGTP	I get the point!
BRB	(I will) be right back	IIRC	If I remember correctly...
BTDT	Been there, done that!	IM(H)O	In my (humble) opinion
BTW	By the way	IOW	In other words...
EG	Evil grin	IRL	In real life...
EL	Evil laugh	ISTR	I seem to remember...
FWIW	For what it's worth...	IYSWIM	...if you see what I mean
FYI	For your information	J/K	Just kidding!
<G>	Grin	K	Okay
GMTA	Great minds think alike	LMAO	Laughing my a*** off!
HAND	Have a nice day!	LOL	Laughing out loud
HTH	Hope this helps	NRN	No reply necessary
IANAL	I am not a lawyer (but)...	OIC	Oh, I see!

OOI	Out of interest...		**WRT**	With regard to...
OTOH	On the other hand...		**WTF**	What the f***?
RO(T)FL	Rolling on (the) floor, laughing		**WTG**	Way to go!
RTFM	Read the f***ing manual!		**YMMV**	Your mileage may vary (i.e. you may get different results)
TTFN	Ta-ta for now		**YW**	You're welcome!
TTYL	Talk to you later		**ZZZ**	Sleeping / bored / tired
WB	Welcome back!			

Online games tend to attract additional abbreviations – for example, card gamers may use **NH** for 'nice hand' and **WP** for 'well played'.

Some people use **HAHA** to indicate laughing. For some reason, I find this deeply annoying. **IMHO** the phrase **LOL** is preferable, but **YMMV**!

❧ Appendix B – Netiquette ❧ for Internet service providers

This section is provided as an appendix because these rules are oriented towards the administrators of ISPs rather than their end-users.

155. Provide users with spam- and virus-filters for their email.

Some users are not willing or able to install software to protect their PCs from these threats. You can mitigate this by offering server-side filtering of emails. However, you should ensure that your users are aware that their messages are being filtered, and allow them to turn off this service if they wish to.

156. Be proactive in identifying compromised computers and notifying the administrators.

If you see a sudden jump in the number of emails being sent from a server, it could indicate that it is being used to send spam or to distribute email viruses. If a server is making an excessive number of attempts to log on to some other server, it could have been compromised by a hacker who is attempting to gain access to other computers by brute-force attacks trying to guess passwords.

By taking swift, proactive steps, you can make your network less attractive to hackers and spammers and can reduce the bandwidth wasted as a result of their actions. Your users will (or, at least, should) welcome being alerted to security problems with their computers.

157. **Encourage your users to adopt practices that will protect the network from abuse.**

For example, support and promote those schemes (such as Yahoo!'s DomainKeys (Yahoo!, 2006) and Microsoft's Sender ID (Microsoft Corporation, 2006)) that authenticate the source of emails and thereby help to reduce spam.

❧ Appendix C – Summary ❧ of rules

Email

1. Each line should be a maximum of 65 characters wide. [Page 10]

2. Structure your message using paragraphs and sentences of sensible lengths. [Page 10]

3. Avoid non-standard forms of English, such as txt or l33t. [Page 10]

4. If you have a signature automatically appended to every email you send, keep its length to a maximum of six (preferably four) lines of 70 characters each. [Page 12]

5. Use an appropriate level of small talk. [Page 14]

6. Keep business emails short and to the point. [Page 15]

7. Think carefully before sending an email that could embarrass you if it were to be more widely distributed. [Page 15]

8. Do not use email to send bad news. [Page 15]

9. Do not write all in capital (or all in lower-case) letters. [Page 16]

10. Do not use email as a way to avoid social interaction. [Page 17]

11. Read your emails before you send them. [Page 17]

12. If your email system allows you to set the priority of the emails you send, make use of this facility (in particular, mark low-priority emails). [Page 18]

13. Wrap URLs in angle brackets, like this: <http://www.example.com/whatever.html>. [Page 18]

14. Take care when using terms that might get your message misidentified as spam. [Page 18]

15. Use a sufficiently long subject so that people will have an accurate idea about your email's contents. [Page 19]

16. Only change subject lines when it is helpful to other people to do so (using [long] and [was ...]). [Page 19]

17. Send messages to only those people who are likely to want to read them. [Page 20]

18. Avoid using BCC unless it is clear that you have done so. [Page 22]

19. Differentiate between TO and CC. [Page 22]

20. Use people's full names (in title case) as well as their email addresses in the TO, FROM and CC fields. [Page 22]

21. Respond promptly to emails sent to you. [Page 23]

22. Use the Reply button in your email software to reply to emails – don't start a new message. [Page 23]

23. Check with the author before adding extra recipients to a reply to an email. [Page 24]

24. It is traditional to include the text of the original message in the reply, typically below the new material and distinguished in some way (such as by prepending each line with a > character). If you need to respond point-by-point, you may intersperse your comments with the original text so long as it is clear which is which. [Page 24]

25. Unless you are adding further recipients to your reply, quote only as much material as is necessary to give context to your own response. [Page 25]

26. If you set up an automatic reply for when you are on holiday, make certain that it will reply only to individuals and not to mailing lists of which you are a member. [Page 25]

27. If you received an email because you were BCCed on it, and other recipients would be surprised that you had seen it, do not use 'Reply to All'. [Page 25]

28. Don't reply to an email just as an easy way to create a new email to the same people. [Page 26]

29. When replying to emails, don't send identical files back to people who already have them. [Page 26]

30. Prepend the subject lines of your replies and forwarded messages with the standard two-letter designations (RE and FW respectively). [Page 26]

31. Always add a short comment to say why you are forwarding the email. [Page 27]

32. Don't forward emails that were sent to you privately (or to a private forum of which you are a member) without the original sender's permission. This applies whether you want to send the email to another person or to a mailing list. [Page 27]

33. Do not edit the text of a forwarded email. [Page 28]

34. Never send warnings about the latest virus by email. [Page 28]

35. Never participate in chain letters. [Page 29]

36. Do not forward jokes or other incidental emails indiscriminately to your friends. [Page 30]

37. Don't email lots of people using raw names in the 'To' box. Instead, use a distribution list or BCC. [Page 31]

38. Send your emails in plain text unless you need to use formatting to benefit your recipients. [Page 32]

39. Don't send attachments at all unless you need to. [Page 33]

40. If you need to send people a large file (say a megabyte or more), contact them first to check how and when they would like to receive it. Don't just send it as an attachment to an email. [Page 33]

41. If you are sending photos, reduce their dimensions. [Page 34]

42. Compress files before you send them to someone else over the Internet. [Page 34]

43. Do not read other people's private emails. [Page 35]

44. Don't use features of your email client that will notify you when someone receives or opens an email that you have sent. [Page 35]

Forums

45. Lurk before you leap! [Page 37]

46. Keep your postings on-topic if possible. [Page 38]

47. If you need to discuss two or more separate topics, post a separate message for each. [Page 39]

48. If you post a disproportionately long message, indicate this in the subject line, for example by appending '[long]'. [Page 39]

49. If you post a message that gives away the ending of a film, book, etc. then clearly mark it as a spoiler in the subject line. [Page 39]

50. Don't post private messages in public forums. [Page 40]

51. If you send a private message to a mailing list by mistake, apologise to both the intended recipient and the group. [Page 40]

52. Do not send a test message to a mailing list. [Page 40]

53. Thank the individual, not the forum. [Page 41]

54. If you post a question and get no response, try some other approach. [Page 41]

55. In contrast to emails, where new material should be at the top, your response should come below the relevant part of the message to which you are replying. [Page 42]

56. Provide an attribution (such as 'On 3 July 2006 Bob Widget wrote:') before any material you quote. [Page 42]

57. Read the whole thread (so far) before posting a reply. [Page 42]

58. Don't reply to someone's opinion simply to agree with them (no 'me too' messages). [Page 42]

59. When replying to a message, reply to the mailing list, not the individual. [Page 43]

60. Keep your posting frequency for replies roughly in sync with that of the other members of the mailing list. [Page 43]

61. Once a thread has run its course, avoid reopening it unless you are genuinely adding useful and relevant information to it. [Page 44]

62. Do not encourage cheating by giving answers to questions that have clearly been set as homework for a course. [Page 44]

63. Don't quote the whole digest when replying. [Page 45]

64. When replying to a digest, change the subject line to match the specific message you are responding to. [Page 45]

65. Don't ask people to reply off-list just because you are a digest subscriber. [Page 46]

66. Do not post a message to a mailing list asking to be unsubscribed. [Page 46]

67. Don't let your inbox overflow when you go on holiday. [Page 47]

68. Before asking a question, check to see if a similar question has been answered before. [Page 49]

69. Don't post announcements about major news events to newsgroups. [Page 49]

70. Do not post any form of attachment to a newsgroup that doesn't have 'binaries' in the name. [Page 50]

71. Do not cross-post any message to more than 10 newsgroups. [Page 50]

72. Use proper cross-posting instead of sending a separate message to each newsgroup. [Page 50]

73. Do not post the same message too often. [Page 51]

74. If you feel that you must invalidate your email address in some way, so as to avoid receiving spam, make sure that the resulting email address is not valid for some other domain. [Page 51]

75. Set expiry dates where appropriate. [Page 52]

76. Allow your messages to be archived. [Page 53]

Real-time messaging

77. Unlike in email messages, it can be permissible to write real-time messages entirely or mainly in lower case. [Page 56]

78. When initiating a chat, check that it is a convenient time for the other person. [Page 56]

79. Set your online status to reflect accurately whether you are available for chat, busy or away. [Page 57]

80. Don't impose your colour scheme on other people. [Page 57]

81. Don't assume that the other person is using the same software. [Page 57]

82. It is acceptable to use standard IM abbreviations, but be prepared to explain any that the other person doesn't understand. [Page 58]

83. Write lots of short messages instead of fewer longer ones. [Page 58]

84. If you have to leave the keyboard unexpectedly and you are in conversation, let the other person know. [Page 59]

85. You may stay logged in to a channel even if you are ignoring the conversation. [Page 60]

86. Use a unique handle. [Page 60]

87. Try to stay on topic. [Page 61]

World Wide Web

88. Do not use a pre-fetching web accelerator. [Page 63]

89. Do use your browser's disk and memory caches. [Page 63]

90. Do not use your employer's equipment to access materials not directly related to your work. [Page 64]

91. Email interesting links to friends manually, not by clicking hyperlinks on websites. [Page 64]

92. Remember your obligations under international copyright laws. [Page 65]

93. If you make files available for download, check them for viruses. [Page 65]

94. If your website contains adult themes, add metatags to rate the content. [Page 65]

95. You do not need permission to link to another web page or website; however, you must not misrepresent the target site when you link. [Page 66]

96. If you need to use an image or other file on your website, add it to your site rather than embedding the file directly from another website. [Page 67]

97. Do not make links open in new pages for no reason. [Page 67]

98. Don't create a website that will only work with a particular sort of browser or size of window. [Page 68]

99. If you need to use advanced features, let them degrade gracefully. [Page 68]

100. Make your web pages accessible to users with disabilities. [Page 69]

101. Check that your web pages conform strictly to the appropriate standards for the technologies they use. [Page 69]

102. Do not automatically resize the browser window. [Page 69]

103. It is perfectly acceptable to present an email address on your website in such a way that it cannot be harvested by spambots. [Page 70]

104. Don't use tactics designed to boost your search engine ranking artificially. This includes, but is not limited to, using fake keywords (including the names of your competitors), gateway pages and dummy articles. [Page 70]

105. Do not allow search engines to index pages that normal users have to pay to access. [Page 71]

Blogs and wikis

106. Only create a blog if you really need one. [Page 73]

107. Take extreme care if writing a blog about your employer. [Page 73]

108. Cite the source of any information you use in your blog. [Page 74]

109. Check the spelling and grammar of your blog posts. [Page 75]

110. Post regularly if possible. [Page 75]

111. Protect against blog spam. [Page 75]

112. Do not participate in an edit war. [Page 76]

113. Do not use public wikis for marketing or self-promotion. [Page 78]

114. Add keywords as links, even if the target subjects do not yet exist. [Page 78]

Transferring files

115. Use a download manager. [Page 81]

116. Use a local mirror if there is one. Download large files off-peak when possible. [Page 81]

117. If an FTP server allows anonymous access, it is polite to use 'anonymous' as the user name and to provide your email address as the password. [Page 82]

118. Peer-to-peer networks are not outside the law. [Page 83]

119. Use a torrent, if available, for large downloads. [Page 83]

120. After downloading via a torrent, leave your BitTorrent client open until you have shared back at least as much data as you downloaded (i.e. until your share ratio is greater than 1.0). [Page 84]

Online auctions

121. Do not bid on an item unless you intend to buy it. [Page 85]

122. Check before you bid that the seller will deliver to your location and will accept a form of payment that you can supply. If you have a question for a seller, ask it before you bid. [Page 85]

123. Leave honest feedback – positive or negative, as appropriate – after each transaction. [Page 85]

Other online services

124. When viewing or listening to streaming media (such as online television, video on demand or radio) use the lowest acceptable quality settings. [Page 87]

125. Don't call people at random unless they have indicated that they wish to receive such calls. [Page 87]

126. Don't use VoIP unless you need an immediate response. [Page 88]

127. Do not register a domain name that a single organisation is likely to want – the name, or a close variant, of the organisation or one of its products – with the intention of trying to sell it to them. [Page 88]

128. Do not make excessive (typically automated) use of free online services. [Page 89]

Advertising and spam

129. Don't send spam. [Page 94]

130. Don't respond to spam. [Page 95]

131. Never use pop-up or pop-under advertisement. [Page 98]

132. Do not use graphical adverts that are designed to look as if they are interactive. [Page 99]

Security

133. Make sure you have a virus scanner, keep its virus definition files up to date, and run scans regularly. [Page 102]

134. Enable macro virus protection in your office software suite. [Page 102]

135. Don't open email attachments unless they were sent from someone you know and you were expecting the attached files. [Page 102]

136. Make sure that you have a firewall installed that checks both inbound and outbound Internet traffic. [Page 103]

137. If your organisation sends emails to customers, make it a policy never to include hyperlinks to your website's logon pages, and make sure that your customers know this. [Page 104]

138. If you receive a phishing email, forward it with full headers to the organisation that is being targeted. [Page 104]

139. Do not send confidential information, such as credit card numbers, by email unless you encrypt it first. [Page 105]

Miscellany

140. Use correct spelling and grammar. [Page 109]

141. Do not post a message just to correct someone else's spelling or grammar mistakes. [Page 109]

142. If you need to include URLs that people are likely to type in, consider providing a shortened version. It is best to provide the full expanded URL as well, unless space in your publication is particularly tight. [Page 110]

143. If you frequently use an online resource that depends on user contributions, contribute. [Page 110]

144. If you need to post something controversial, wrap it between <flame> and </flame> tags. [Page 112]

145. Do not troll. [Page 112]

146. Do not respond to trolls. [Page 113]

147. On Usenet, keep discussions about the respective merits of competing technologies to the 'advocacy' newsgroups in the 'comp' hierarchy. [Page 113]

148. If you feel that a misunderstanding via email has brought you to the brink of a flame war with someone you know, do not try to use email to resolve the situation. Instead, meet face to face or call them on the telephone. [Page 113]

149. If you have said or done something wrong, apologise. [Page 114]

150. Run wireless networking equipment at the lowest power you need. [Page 115]

151. Consider the environmental effect of the way you use your computer. [Page 115]

152. Use your computer to reduce the amount of waste paper you produce. [Page 116]

153. Dispose of old computer equipment in an environmentally responsible way. [Page 116]

154. Never give out your personal details in online chatrooms. [Page 116]

Netiquette for Internet service providers

155. Provide users with spam- and virus-filters for their email. [Page 123]

156. Be proactive in identifying compromised computers and notifying the administrators. [Page 123]

157. Encourage your users to adopt practices that will protect the network from abuse. [Page 124]

Glossary

This glossary provides a quick way to look up the meaning of any technical words that have been used in this book. Words appearing in **bold face** in the descriptions have glossary entries of their own, to which you may like to refer for additional information.

419 fraud

a type of **advance fee fraud** in which someone is conned into believing that they are to transfer a large sum of money between countries; it is named after the section of the Nigerian criminal code relating to it

abbreviation

an **acronym**, **initialism** or other form of shortened word or phrase

acronym

an **initialism** that is itself a pronounceable word

advance fee fraud

a scam where someone is conned out of a sum of money because of the promise of a much larger sum to come

anonymous FTP

an **FTP** server that allows free access (i.e. without needing to set up an account)

ASCII

the American Standard Code for Information Interchange – a code for representing letters, digits, punctuation and so on as numbers for encoding on computers

ASCII art

pictures made from a grid of fixed-width **ASCII** symbols

bandwidth

the maximum capacity for transferring data over a network

BCC	blind carbon copy – a list of people who should receive a copy of an email without other recipients being able to see that they have received it (see also **CC**)
BitTorrent	a **peer-to-peer** downloading program and its associated protocol
blog	a 'web log' – an online diary or journal of thoughts
browser	software used for surfing the World Wide Web, such as Microsoft Internet Explorer or Mozilla Firefox
cache	a local copy of frequently-requested remote data – a web browser can use a cache of visited web pages so that they load more quickly if the user decides to return to them
CAPTCHA™	Completely Automated Public Turing test to tell Computers and Humans Apart – a picture of a word that has been altered so that people can read it but computers cannot
CC	carbon copy – a list of people who should receive an email in addition to the main recipients (see also **BCC**)
checksum	a short value generated from a larger one (even an entire file) to check that it has been received correctly (see also **MD5 checksum**)
cross-posting	posting a **Usenet** message to more than one newsgroup at a time (see also **ECP**)
cyber-squatting	the action of registering a **domain name** that ought rightfully to belong to someone else, with a view to selling it to them for a high price

domain name	a textual representation of a particular computer on the Internet, such as 'example.com'
dooced	to be fired from your job as a result of posting messages about them on your **blog** (see page 74)
download manager	software that will let you resume downloading a file if your connection is lost part-way through, so you don't have to start again from the beginning
ECP	excessive cross-posting (posting the same message to too many different groups, typically in **Usenet**)
edit war	a disagreement between two factions editing a **wiki**, each deleting the other's changes in a never-ending cycle
emoticon	a sequence of characters designed to express emotion in informal written text, such as :-) to represent a smile
EMP	excessive multi-posting (posting too many copies of the same article, typically in **Usenet**)
FAQ	frequently asked question(s) – a fundamental topic; lists of FAQs are compiled so that people don't keep having to ask the same questions on a forum
firewall	a hardware or software device that applies security rules to prevent certain traffic from passing between networks
flame	an insulting personal comment made in anger
flamebait	a comment made by a **troll** to encourage someone to **flame**, or made accidentally but still likely to result in flames

143

flame war	an online discussion that has broken down to the extent that it is little more than a series of personal attacks
FTP	File Transfer Protocol
FW	the two-letter designation used at the start of an email's subject line to indicate that it is a forwarded email (see also **RE**)
GUI	graphical user interface – the windows and icons you use to interact with your computer
hacker	someone with a deep interest in how technology works – used in this book in the more restrictive sense of someone who accesses computer networks without permission
handle	a nickname used on **IRC**
HTML	HyperText Markup Language – the code used to create web pages
HTML email	A message formatted as HTML and sent as an attachment to an email.
HTTP	HyperText Transfer Protocol – the networking protocol used for transferring **HTML** pages between computers
IM	instant messaging – a form of **real-time messaging**, usually supporting lists of contacts
initialism	a word formed from the first letters of the words in a phrase (see also **acronym**)

IRC	Internet Relay Chat – a form of **real-time messaging** using named channels (such as '#linux') for communication amongst people interested in a particular topic
ISP	Internet Service Provider – a company that connects people to the Internet
JavaScript	a programming language, supported by most web browsing software, used mainly to add dynamic content to web pages
l33t	a simple cipher in which letters are replaced by numbers or other symbols, typically used by **hackers** and wannabe hackers
listserv	a popular mailing-list administration program (see also **majordomo**)
lurking	reading messages posted to a forum without posting any – useful at first, but could be considered to be anti-social if done for a long time
majordomo	a popular mailing-list administration program (see also **listserv**)
malware	any software that deliberately causes harm to computer systems (see also **Trojan horse, spyware, worm** and **virus**)
MD5 checksum	a particular type of **checksum** comprising 16 hexadecimal digits
megapixel	one million **pixels**
metatag	an **HTML** tag that holds information about a web page

mirror	a complete copy of a website or **FTP** server, typically located in a different part of the world; mirrors can increase download speeds and help to reduce the network traffic for the main server
mung(e)	to corrupt something irrevocably; typically refers to email addresses that have been deliberately altered to prevent **spambots** from being able to use them (such as 'myDELETETHISaddress@ANDTHIS.example.com')
netiquette	network etiquette – behaving online with civility
Network News	another name for **Usenet**
newbie	a new (and therefore inexperienced) user
newsgroup	a discussion forum on **Usenet**
one-click hoster	a website that acts as a service for transferring large files
peer-to-peer network	a network of computers in which each is free to connect directly to the others (instead of having to connect via a designated server computer)
phishing	the illegal practice of setting up clones of real websites for the purpose of stealing usernames and passwords from users; this is typically done by sending fake emails to banking customers
ping back	an automatic comment appended to a **blog** message when someone links to it from another **blog**
pixel	a 'picture element' – one coloured dot in a digital image
port	a numbered virtual device through which connections between computers are made

postmaster	the person who administers an organisation's email system
pyramid scheme	a fraud in which newcomers to the scheme must pay money to existing members in order that people who join later will pay money to them
RE	the two-letter designation used at the start of an email's subject line to indicate that it is a reply to a previous email (see also **FW**)
real-time messaging	instantaneous typed communication between people over the Internet – examples are **IRC** and **IM**
seeder	someone who makes a file available for download via **BitTorrent**
sig	a signature at the bottom of an email message, giving contact details etc.
smiley	another word for **emoticon**
snip	a tag used to indicate that an unimportant part of an email has been deliberately removed in a reply
sniping	bidding on an online auction just before it closes, so that other bidders do not have time to outbid you
spam	unsolicited commercial email
spambot	software that trawls an Internet system, such as **Usenet** or the World Wide Web, looking for email addresses on behalf of a spammer
spoiler	information that reveals a plot twist that could spoil someone's enjoyment of a book or film they have not yet seen

spyware	**malware** designed to watch users without their consent and report their actions back to a third party
thread	a group of messages about a single topic
top-posting	adding new material before quoted text – frowned upon on **Usenet**
torrent	another name for **BitTorrent**
Trojan horse	non-replicating **malware** that typically undermines the security of a computer system, allowing hackers to gain access
troll	someone who deliberately posts **flamebait** just to get a reaction
txt	a form of concise communication favoured in SMS text messages, and used by some in informal **real-time messaging**
URL	uniform resource locator – typically a web address such as 'http://www.w3.org'
Usenet	a network of servers that allow subscribers to read and post messages to **newsgroups**
virus	a form of **malware** that is embedded in another program and can replicate and spread, infecting other computers
VoIP	Voice over Internet Protocol – a way of making telephone calls over the Internet
W3C	World Wide Web Consortium – the governing body of the Web, which develops the official standards for interoperability

wiki	a website that anyone can make changes to online; the most famous wiki is Wikipedia.com, an online encyclopaedia, but there are thousands of others
worm	self-contained **malware** that attempts to copy itself over a network
XHTML	a version of **HTML** coded using extensible markup language (XML)
zip	a file format for compressed files

Bibliography

Agre, P. (1994, February). *The Art of Getting Help*. Retrieved August 4, 2006, from http://polaris.gseis.ucla.edu/pagre/getting-help.html

Armstrong, H. (2006, November 28). *Dooce.com*. Retrieved November 29, 2006, from http://www.dooce.com

Baseley, W. D. (1999, August 8). *Address Munging FAQ: "Spam-Blocking" Your Email Address*. Retrieved November 1, 2006, from http://members.aol.com/emailfaq/mungfaq.html

BBC (2002, August 16). *Examiner's Warning Over Exams Culture*. Retrieved October 17, 2006, from BBC News: http://news.bbc.co.uk/1/hi/education/2197173.stm

BBC (2003, March 4). *Is txt Mightier than the Word?* Retrieved October 17, 2006, from BBC News: http://news.bbc.co.uk/1/hi/uk/2814235.stm

Bechtold, S. (2004, July). *Link Controversy Page*. Retrieved July 26, 2006, from http://www.jura.uni-tuebingen.de/bechtold/lcp.html

Belbin, R. M. (2003). *Management Teams – Why They Succeed or Fail* (second edition). Butterworth Heinemann.

Berners-Lee, T. (1997, April). *Links and Law: Myths*. Retrieved July 25, 2006, from http://www.w3.org/DesignIssues/LinkMyths.html

Brouwer, S., & Bryan, A. (2006, February). *Using MD5 Checksums*. Retrieved November 5, 2006, from OpenOffice.org: http://www.openoffice.org/dev_docs/using_md5sums.html

Craddock, A. (1997, July 10). *Spamming Lawyer Disbarred*. Retrieved October 22, 2006, from Wired News: http://www.wired.com/news/politics/0,1283,5060,00.html

Crocker, D. (1997, May). *Mailbox Names for Common Services, Roles and Functions*. Retrieved October 11, 2006, from http://www.rfc-editor.org/rfc/rfc2142.txt

Eastlake, D., & Panitz, A. (1999, June). *Reserved Top Level DNS Names*. Retrieved July 26, 2006, from ftp://ftp.frc-editor.org/in-notes/rfc2606.txt

Electronic Frontier Foundation (n.d.). *EFF Needs Your Support in the Fight for Bloggers' Rights!* Retrieved November 29, 2006, from EFF: http://www.eff.org/bloggers/join

Flynn, N. *Blog Rules: A Business Guide to Managing Policy, Public Relations, and Legal Issues.* New York: AMACOM.

Google (2006, October 22). *Google AdWords.* Retrieved October 22, 2006, from Google: https://adwords.google.com

Hambridge, S., & Intel (1995, October). RFC1855 (*Netiquette Guidelines*).

Harris, D. (2006, January 23). *Etiquette Guidelines for Electronic Mail.* Retrieved August 15, 2006, from http://www.pmail.com/etqtte.htm

Henricson, M., & Nyquist, E. (1992, April 27). *Programming in C++, Rules and Recommendations.* (J. Supanich, Trans.) Älvsjö, Sweden: Ellemtel Telecommunication Systems Laboratories. Retrieved August 12, 2006, from http://www.doc.ic.ac.uk/lab/cplus/c++.rules

Horton, M., Spafford, G., & Moraes, M. (1998, January 16). *Rules for Posting to Usenet.* Retrieved July 24, 2006, from ftp://ftp.faqs.org/faqs/usenet/posting-rules/part1

ibiblio (1999, February 10). *Logs of Major Events in the Online Community.* Retrieved October 22, 2006, from http://www.ibiblio.org/pub/academic/communications/logs

Internet Watch Foundation (2006, September 18). Safe Surfing Links. Retrieved November 27, 2006, from Internet Watch Foundation: http://www.iwf.org.uk/public/page.92.htm

Kallos, J. (2004). *Because Netiquette Matters!* Philadelphia, PA: Xlibris Corporation.

Leavitt, T. (Ed.). (n.d.). *The Canter & Siegel Report, Number One.* Retrieved October 22, 2006, from ftp://ftp.armory.com/pub/user/leavitt/html/cands.report.html

Leiner, B. M., Cerf, V. G., Clark, D. D., et al. (2003, December 10). *A Brief History of the Internet.* Retrieved October 13, 2006, from Internet Society: http://www.isoc.org/internet/history/brief.shtml

McCarthy, K. (2001, February 28). *SMS: Sack Me Surruptitiously.* Retrieved October 11, 2006, from http://www.theregister.co.uk/2001/02/28/sms_sack_me_surruptitiously

Microsoft Corporation (2006, November 5). *Sender ID.* Retrieved November 5, 2006, from Microsoft: http://www.microsoft.com/mscorp/safety/technologies/senderid/default.mspx

Morgan, J. (1996). *Debrett's New Guide to Etiquette & Modern Manners.* London: Headline Book Publishing.

Open Directory Project (2006, September 12). *Computers : Software : Internet : Clients : Usenet.* Retrieved November 1, 2006, from Open Directory Project: http://dmoz.org/Computers/Software/Internet/Clients/Usenet

Shea, V. (1994). *Netiquette.* San Francisco: Albion Books.

Sifry, D. (2006, November 6). *State of the Blogosphere, October, 2006.* Retrieved November 28, 2006, from Sifry's Alerts: http://www.sifry.com/alerts/archives/000443.html

Simonetti, E. (2006, November 28). *Diary of a Fired Flight Attendant.* Retrieved November 29, 2006, from http://queenofsky.journalspace.com

Skirvin, T. (2004, May 16). *FAQ: Current Usenet Spam Thresholds and Guidelines.* Retrieved July 24, 2006, from http://www.faqs.org/faqs/usenet/spam-faq

Spyware Warrior (2006, October 23). *The Spyware Warrior List of Rogue/Suspect Anti-Spyware Products & Web Sites.* Retrieved November 3, 2006, from Spyware Warrior: http://spywarewarrior.com/rogue_anti-spyware.htm

Templeton, B. (1999, December 28). *Emily Postnews Answers Your Questions on Netiquette.* Retrieved July 7, 2006, from http://www.faqs.org/faqs/usenet/emily-postnews/part1

Templeton, B. (2005, March 21). *Reaction to the DEC Spam of 1978.* Retrieved October 22, 2006, from Brad Templeton's Home Page: http://www.templetons.com/brad/spamreact.html

W3C Web Accessibility Initiative (n.d.). *Web Content Accessibility Guidelines.* Retrieved July 25, 2006, from http://www.w3.org/WAI/intro/wcag.php

Wikipedia (2006, November 28). *Wikiquette*. Retrieved December 5, 2006, from Wikipedia: http://en.wikipedia.org/wiki/Wikipedia:Wikiquette

Wikipedia (2006, December 5). *Leet*. Retrieved October 17, 2006, from Wikipedia: http://en.wikipedia.org/wiki/Leet

Yahoo! (2006, November 5). *DomainKeys*. Retrieved November 5, 2006, from Yahoo! Anti-Spam Resource Center: http://antispam.yahoo.com/domainkeys

Yapp, N. (1994). *Debrett's Guide to Business Etiquette*. London: Headline Book Publishing.

Index

About the author

Matthew Strawbridge is a freelance software engineer, copy editor and technical author living and working in Ely, near Cambridge in the UK. He is the founder of Software Reference Limited. You can find out more about Matthew's work at **http://www.philoxenic.com** and more about Software Reference at **http://www.swref.com**.

Other books by Matthew Strawbridge

BTEC First

BTEC First ICT Practitioners, 2nd Ed. (co-author)
Heinemann Educational Publishers
ISBN: 978 0 435402 04 4

European Computer Driving Licence Advanced Level

Advanced ECDL Word Processing Payne-Gallway Publishers ISBN: 978 1 904467 88 5	*Advanced ECDL Database* Payne-Gallway Publishers ISBN: 978 1 904467 90 8
Advanced ECDL Spreadsheets Payne-Gallway Publishers ISBN: 978 1 904467 89 2	*Advanced ECDL Presentation* Payne-Gallway Publishers ISBN: 978 1 904467 91 5

 # Colophon

The page size is $9'' \times 6''$, and the main text block follows these 3:2 dimensions. The text block including the running heads has a φ:1 ratio, where φ is the golden ratio (approximately 1.618).

This book was typeset in Adobe InDesign CS. Body text uses Adobe Garamond Pro at 11/14. Headings are set in the wonderful **Gill Sans**. Monospaced text uses `Lucida Console`.

This book was printed and distributed by Lightning Source Inc.

Printed in the United Kingdom
by Lightning Source UK Ltd.
129947UK00001B/52-66/A